Assessing Competitive Intelligence Software

A Guide to Evaluating CI Technology

> > >

Assessing
Competitive
Intelligence
Software

> > > A Guide to Evaluating CI Technology

France Bouthillier
and
Kathleen Shearer

Information Today, Inc.
Medford, New Jersey

First printing, 2003

Assessing Competitive Intelligence Software:
A Guide to Evaluating CI Technology

Library of Congress Cataloging-in-Publication Data

Bouthillier, France, 1959–

    Assessing competitive intelligence software : a guide to evaluating CI technology / France Bouthillier and Kathleen Shearer.

       p. cm.

    ISBN 1-57387-173-7 (hardcover)

     1. Business intelligence--Data processing. I. Shearer, Kathleen, 1967- II. Title.

HD38.7.B684 2003

    658.4'7'02855--dc21

                                  2003011847

Publisher: Thomas H. Hogan, Sr.
Editor-in-Chief: John B. Bryans
Managing Editor: Deborah R. Poulson
Graphics Department Director: M. Heide Dengler
Copy Editor: Dorothy Pike
Book Designer: Kara Mia Jalkowski
Cover Designer: Laura Hegyi
Indexer: Sharon Hughes

Contents

CHAPTER 1
Value-Addedness and Information: Two Notions, One Goal 1

CHAPTER 2
A Conceptual Framework for Competitive Intelligence 23

CHAPTER 3
Identifying the Value-Added Processes of
Competitive Intelligence 57

CHAPTER 4
**Overview of Competitive Intelligence Software
Applications and Related Products 83**

CHAPTER 5
Evaluating Competitive Intelligence Software 109

Figures

Tables

Foreword

Organizations today thrive in turbulent times. Not so long ago, when environments were relatively stable, organizations kept their eyes on internal operations. The defining feature of managerial success then was decision making. As environments become increasingly volatile, organizations are turning their gaze to the external horizon, watching and grappling with a confusion of signals, messages, and cues. The defining core of managerial work now is to know what is going on in order to be able to decide what is to be done. Sensing and making sense of the environment have become the sine qua non for organizational growth and survival.

Sensing the environment is to gather information about events, relationships, and trends in a firm's external world. This is much harder than it sounds because of the rapid pace of change, the ambiguity of signals and messages, and the density of relationships among actors and stakeholders. Making sense of equivocal signals and messages is an even greater challenge: The question is not only whether we are getting enough information about the environment, but what does the information we are noticing mean. As a result, an effective competitive intelligence (CI) process must embrace two sets of strategic concerns: to collect information about the competitive environment that captures the richness and complexity of the arena that the firm is in, and to interpret the information so as to develop an understanding of the environment that will enable the firm to act to strengthen its competitive position and to avoid being blindsided or caught by surprise.

In an increasingly munificent information world, what would be the role of information technology in the CI process? What leverage can IT bring to the CI process? How does an organization choose from a bewildering range of IT tools in order to amplify its CI capabilities? How does a firm interface and integrate the use of IT with the human and social processes that lie at the heart of turning information into intelligence? These are the fundamental questions that the book seeks to answer.

This book makes two important contributions. First, it constructs a conceptual model of CI that is based on a clear and distinctive analysis of the underlying information processes driving the CI cycle. The model describes the processes in detail and draws out concrete suggestions about how each of these processes should be managed. The guiding principle is to view information processes as value-adding processes. Paradoxically, what one organization sees as highly relevant information, another organization might regard as noise and distraction. The book resolves this conundrum by systematically examining the various ways that information becomes valuable to an individual or organization. The conceptual model presented here represents a significant achievement that builds upon the theoretical foundations of information science and the practical experience of the CI profession.

A second major contribution is the development of a useful framework for evaluating CI software platforms. A set of 32 evaluation criteria is carefully derived from the earlier analysis of the value-adding information processes that make up the CI cycle. This framework is then applied step by step in a comparative evaluation of four major CI software packages. The general conclusion of the evaluation is that these software packages can indeed add value to the CI cycle. However there are a few caveats. Each package has its own strengths, emphasizing different component processes of the cycle. None of the packages seems to support the full CI cycle completely. A common limitation is that the software does not support the analysis and interpretation process adequately. Moreover, a significant investment in learning, administration and maintenance is required to use these systems.

At a more general level, the book calls to attention some basic issues concerning the role of information technology in supporting the information work of an organization. Specifically, there are some implicit tensions in applying information technology to support the flow of CI activity. IT can be used to gather a larger quantity of information, but this information volume needs to be managed lest it becomes overwhelming. One way to do this is to define information needs formally, but sometimes information needs are hard to predefine but are revealed by scanning broadly and noticing connections serendipitously. IT can be efficient in organizing and presenting information, but sometimes at the price of losing something of the context and nuance that is so important in interpreting ambiguous information about a fluid environment. IT can analyze information in ways that a person cannot: Large amounts of data may be mined to look for clusters and patterns; simulations may be run to project trends or outcomes. At the same time, the assessment of the meaning and significance of these results remains a human endeavor fraught with difficulty.

This book takes an important step in helping us understand the interaction between information technology and information work in organizations. It illuminates the complex interplay between the information efficiency that is promised by the application of information technology and the information effectiveness that comes from a clear understanding of how people in organizations seek and shape information into action and purpose.

Chun Wei Choo
Faculty of Information Studies
University of Toronto

Preface

Osama bin Laden! Terrorism! Before September 11, 2001, very few people in the world could relate the name and the word. Today, the whole planet shares that information: The name, the word, and the date are linked forever. Since then, many people have come to realize that having large amounts of information does not necessarily translate into having intelligence. In our so-called information society, knowing what to do with information—how to treat it, how to analyze it, and how to use it—is an even more difficult task, mastered by few. In today's society, with the increasingly rapid distribution of information, we not only face information overload, which can paralyze action, but also potential disinterest in information, leading to an indifference toward the value of information. Twenty years ago, reporting about the bombing of a U.S. marine base in Beirut, the *New York Times* stated that "so much raw intelligence on possible terrorist threats poured in that, after a while, the marines stopped taking all of it seriously. The problem in Beirut was not insufficient information, but a lack of trained analysts to evaluate it" (the *New York Times*, December 11, 1983, p. 49). Numerous examples like this remind us that the problem of the improper handling of information is not new and that consequences of mishandling information can be grave. Information overload affects all types of organizations, including governments and businesses.

Organizations also suffer from a lack of intelligence, and lack of analysis of its implications. In the past 20 years, we have seen a shift from the information-based society to the knowledge-based society. This shift reflects a growing understanding that the value of information is directly related to whether it contributes to the state of knowing. In other words, information itself has no value unless something is learned from its use.

In business, the development of a project may encounter numerous obstacles along the way. Legal, industrial, technological, financial, and market constraints abound. A lack of information or, worse, the absence of intelligence about these various aspects can be a major obstacle. For many enterprises, it is easy to obtain information about competitors. Knowing how to interpret this information, to understand its significance and its potential impact on the industry and the organization is less easy, and it requires time and expertise.

Doing business without tracking competitors is extremely risky. The globalization of markets accompanied by rapid changes in technology have increased the competitiveness in most industries. The fact is that information-related activities are now deemed to be critical success factors within organizations. In the struggle to remain competitive, many companies have turned to new technologies to improve their business activities. This development is also true for information-related activities, in which technology has traditionally been used to accomplish numerous tasks. As technologies evolve and change to fulfill these growing needs, organizations need to examine them closely and assess their role and value within the organization.

The general purpose of this book is to help clarify the difference between information and intelligence. Indeed, there is a fine line between both. One cannot consult business information sources today, where information is presented as a critical asset, without encountering endlessly the term "Competitive Intelligence" (CI). Every year, numerous books, articles, and Web sites devoted to this topic are made available. Searching the phrase "competitive intelligence" on the Web search engine Google yields more than 500,000 Web pages where the term can be found. In addition, a growing number of companies offer business intelligence and competitive intelligence solutions. These innovative tools raise a fundamental question: Are they useful for collecting information for business purposes or for implementing an intelligence process? That question is difficult to answer without a thorough analysis of the tools' features.

Globalization has had a profound effect on the business activities required to remain competitive, making CI increasingly attractive. Unfortunately, most people refer to CI in general terms that do not clearly communicate what they really have in mind, a problem especially evident when dealing with those who design particular software applications for the purpose of CI. It is interesting, however, to discover the wide variety of meanings attributed to CI. Authors offer a diversity of definitions; publications describe various approaches, practices, techniques, or tools from different angles; and technologies are developed to address multiple CI needs. A plethora of similar terms are also used: business intelligence, competitor intelligence, market intelligence, competitor targeting, environmental scanning, and others. The conceptual differences between them are not always obvious and are in fact muddled even more by experts who in some cases develop their own terminology.

What is competitive intelligence? Basically, it is a process involving a number of information-related activities. CI implies the use of publicly available information to learn various things about competitors. It involves monitoring the environment on a constant basis. But what is the difference between conducting CI and collecting business information? Intelligence is the capacity to know, to understand; it is the exercise of knowing. Gathering information is an important step, but to create intelligence, one must go beyond this step. In this book, we argue that information can only be transformed into intelligence when some value is added, bringing a qualitative change in the nature of the information in order to make it more meaningful and more useful for decision making and action.

One explanation for the growing interest in CI software applications is the boom in available business information sources. Williams (2001), who examined the online database industry for 20 years, reported that in 1975 there were 301 information databases, in comparison to 12,417 databases in 2000, about 41 times more. The number of records contained in these databases was 52 million in 1975 as opposed to nearly 15.25 billion in 2000, corresponding to a growth by a factor of 265. In terms of subject classes, 24 percent of the databases identified in 2000 were related to business. Thus, business represents a larger number of databases than any other subject, including news/general and science/technology/engineering. Given such tremendous growth in the amount of business information, it is not surprising to see a growth in the demand for software to handle it. As a result, the market today offers a variety of software applications aimed at providing assistance to organizations for implementing and organizing CI activities. These tools are presented as useful for managing the entire CI function, while, in fact, they might manage only a small part of the CI process or they might address tasks that are connected to other business areas.

One objective of this book is to provide a framework for assessing CI software, establishing the extent to which these applications can add value to information. Because business information can be easily retrieved from the Web and numerous other sources, accessing or gathering information is no longer a major challenge. As Liautaud (2001) rightly pointed out, organizations can collect so much information in their database infrastructure that it becomes a liability rather than an asset. Indeed, the acquisition and storage costs can become higher than the ultimate value of the information. To generate valuable information, or to add value to information, an information system must facilitate its analysis, its interpretation, and its sharing.

Evaluation studies of CI software exist, but none has been conducted using an information-processing approach. This introduces another objective of the book: to present a conceptual definition of CI by identifying the set of tasks related to the treatment of information in CI. In other words, our goal is to identify the value-added processes inherent to CI. One cannot evaluate the adequacy and relevance of CI software without a clear conceptual model and likewise without a strong understanding of the CI process. A set of evaluation criteria for CI software must correspond with the CI process and its conceptual model. An information-processing approach to CI is useful in that it identifies the various stages through which information must be processed, transforming it into intelligence.

Given the growing interest in CI and new technologies, the need arises for an explicit set of evaluation criteria that potential consumers could use to assess what the technology could do for them. When authors evaluate CI software, they do not always make available to the readers their precise criteria, and the focus is usually on the final ranking of the applications. We use a different approach here. The focus is on presenting a set of evaluation criteria and explaining how these criteria can be used by anyone. The final ranking of software packages emphasizes how the criteria can be applied rather than a definitive evaluation of the software, considering that the technology evolves at such a rapid rate. In addition, we hope that the ranking provided here, based on our perceptions and the information made available by the software producers, will stimulate the debate surrounding CI technology in general and motivate the CI community to reflect about the value of current CI technology.

Therefore, the purpose of the book is not to provide tips and tricks relating to the implementation or maintenance of a CI department or function in an organization. Nor is it to investigate current practices or propose particular approaches or techniques. Our goal is to add to the intellectual foundations of CI. By clarifying the nature of CI through an information-processing perspective, we hope to contribute to the development of a common understanding of how innovative technologies can be used to better support CI activities.

Audience

Although the focus of the book is narrow, it is written for a diversified audience. Information specialists and competitive intelligence professionals need evaluation criteria for sound appraisals of CI software applications, to understand what CI processes a software application performs, to examine the extent to which the software might facilitate their work, to help them to make purchasing decisions, and to more objectively monitor the software market. The business community—in particular small and medium-sized businesses—needs to be better informed about the conceptual and practical differences of existing software applications in order to make sound purchasing decisions. Business people are the obvious targets for companies commercializing these applications, but they do not always have the time or the expertise to compare sophisticated information products. For small businesses, the idea that an application would fulfill all their CI needs is very appealing. Unfortunately, implementing and using new technology can be very time consuming and, without its proper assessment, can be another source of information overload rather than an efficient solution.

Instructors and students of competitive intelligence courses and programs can use this book for discussing the nature of CI activities, for examining the existing CI software market, and for analyzing particular packages. Finally, software designers can benefit from a set of public evaluation criteria to improve and update applications to better meet the requirements of the tasks supposedly addressed by the tools they design.

Organization of the Book

The idea of adding value to information is one of the basic premises in the field of information science. However, the concept of value-addedness is often used in a generic way, lacking a clear definition. In fact, it is quite a troublesome term. Chapter 1 presents a brief review of the literature addressing the idea that information has value and that value can be added to information. The aim is to provide readers with a greater understanding of what information/intelligence professionals and systems should try to achieve when they attempt to add value to information or to provide value-added information services.

Chapter 2 is devoted to the concept of competitive intelligence. This chapter provides the conceptual framework for the management and assessment of competitive intelligence. The intention is not to explain how to conduct CI, but rather to outline what it is, which information-related activities are involved in it, and to discuss some of the ambiguities and overlaps affecting the concept of CI and several related terms such as business intelligence and market intelligence. In this chapter, the information-processing approach to CI is presented and the six major processes involved are described in detail.

Chapter 3 describes 32 evaluation criteria for assessing CI software. Each is related to one of the six information processes described in Chapter 2. The criteria are presented in a way that they can be used by anyone who is interested in purchasing CI software. The chapter provides users with a practical methodology for examining the amount of value added by a software application and identifying in which step of the CI process the value is added.

Chapter 4 discusses the evolution of the CI software market, as well as the various trends in the development of business information technology. The nature of the CI software market to date is extremely inclusive and contains numerous applications, many of which do not perform CI as outlined by our conceptual framework. This chapter presents a typology of technologies associated with CI. The typology categorizes the main types of products that are available on the market and helps to make sense of the technological diversity. The chapter also provides basic selection criteria for identifying legitimate CI software applications and describes, briefly, existing "off-the-shelf" software applications that meet these criteria.

Chapter 5 offers a comparative analysis of several leading CI software applications. This chapter presents an in-depth discussion of the strengths and weaknesses of the software applications based on their ability to add value throughout the entire competitive intelligence process. The intention is to show how an overall assessment can be performed, comparing attributes of a number of packages. These product evaluations seek only to illustrate how our methodology can be used in practice and should not be considered as final evaluations of the products in question. Some of the products were tested in demonstration versions and did not showcase the full functionality of the product. For other products, we relied heavily on the documentation provided by the producers. Thus, our evaluations have many limitations. It is important to note also that new versions of some of these products will be available by the time you read this, with added features that may address some of the weaknesses we encountered.

The book concludes with a summary of the findings of our comparative analysis and recommendations for purchasing and designing CI software applications.

We hope you will find as much value in reading *Assessing Competitive Intelligence Software* as we did in writing it. Please let us know what you think.

France Bouthillier
Kathleen Shearer
france.bouthillier@mcgill.ca

Acknowledgments

The publication of this book would not have been possible without the support and contribution of numerous people. First, we are grateful to our editor, John Bryans, Editor-in-Chief of Information Today Books, and to Deborah Poulson, Managing Editor, for their support and guidance.

Second, we would like to thank Patrizia Gagliardi and Tao Jin, students in the Master in Library and Information Studies at McGill University, who agreed to work with us and helped in the collection of materials and information.

We would also like to thank the software vendors: This project could not have succeeded without their willingness to share with us demos and information about their products.

Finally, a special thanks to our families and friends for their patience and quiet acceptance of the time we spent during evenings, weekends, and nights discussing and writing this book instead of being with them. In particular, Kathleen would like to thank Clement Davis for his support, and France would like to thank Jean Guilbault and their daughter, Laurence.

CHAPTER 1

Value-Addedness and Information: Two Notions, One Goal

The notion that value is added to information as it passes through an information-related system is implied in the expressions "value-added information" or "information with added value," and this is no different for competitive intelligence (CI). But what is value, how can value be added to information, and what types and degrees of added value are necessary for CI?

The terms "information" and "value" convey complex ideas that are not always considered in the competitive intelligence and information science literature. Although the goal of offering value-added information is a legitimate one for CI practitioners, information professionals, and designers of information-related technology alike, this goal is not easy to achieve for a number of reasons. Without a doubt, information and value are not tangible objects that can be delivered and owned. What is information? What is the value of information? How can value be added to information with or without technology? The answers to these questions are of great importance to anyone involved in information-related activities. Competitive intelligence is a costly process, and the cost is only acceptable if its outcomes are of value to the organization. But what kind of value is obtained through CI, and how?

In the business sector, the idea of adding value is well established. To enter and remain in business, an entrepreneur or corporation must add value to an existing resource, product, or service to gain and to maintain a competitive advantage. Discovering a diamond mine does not automatically make an entrepreneur wealthy. Rough diamonds must go through many processes to be transformed into valuable gems. Extracting, transporting, cutting, and polishing rough diamonds are essential steps to obtain a resource that will be marketable and sold to others who will appreciate its value.

Similarly, to obtain information and transform it into something of value, such as CI, a number of processes are essential. However, for most, the idea that information systems, technologies, or services can add value to information is relatively new. For instance, for many centuries libraries have added value to cultural products by organizing collections of manuscripts and books. In spite of the evolution of their information systems and services, their cultural and symbolic roles have often taken precedence over their function of adding value, which has remained obscure for most people. Today, anyone working in the information sector, whether as a publisher, an information provider, or CI professional, knows that adding value to information is absolutely critical. With the development of media and the Internet, information is available in so many formats and from so many sources.

Many aspects are incorporated in adding value to information. At one level, a major value-adding activity is to filter through the mountains of information, identifying what has value and what does not. At another level, value can be augmented through the analysis of information by adding more meaning to it and transforming it into intelligence. But what exactly do we mean by these activities and how are they achieved?

In this chapter, our goal is to define a number of concepts—information and intelligence, as well as data and knowledge—in order to help the reader better understand the nature of the processes that add value to information. The differences, overlaps, and similarities must be examined in order to achieve a more complete understanding of another important concept: value. We will also discuss the value-added processes involved in information systems as identified by Taylor (1986) because they contribute greatly to an understanding of how information is transmuted into intelligence from the user perspective.

From Data to Knowledge

To comprehend the differences between information and intelligence, we need to explore the relationships and overlaps that exist between these two concepts on one hand, and between data and knowledge on the other. It is not our intention here to end the debate about the real nature of these terms but rather to better circumscribe the nature of intelligence, which is a key requirement of any CI system.

The terms "data," "information," "intelligence," and "knowledge" are often presented along a continuum, their links and nuances expressed as a matter of degree rather than kind. When we look more closely at the definitions of these concepts, it is easy to get confused. To some extent information is made of data, knowledge requires information, and intelligence relies on both information and some type of knowledge. Dictionaries define data as factual information—facts, measurements, or statistics—used as a basis for reasoning, discussion, or calculation, while information has several meanings. It is the communication or reception of knowledge or intelligence, thus it is the action of informing. Information is also a piece of knowledge that can be communicated, codified, stored, and retrieved. For some, information is an organized form of data. Knowledge, on the other hand, is described as the condition of knowing something gained through experience and the condition of apprehending truth or fact through reasoning or intuition. Knowledge is organized information that is internalized by its user and integrated in its behavior. Finally, intelligence can be defined as the ability to understand and apply knowledge. Some authors suggest that the attempt to differentiate between these terms is fruitless. Mass (1988), for instance, argues that data, words, records, or whatever it is called remains information and the term information encompasses all the others. It is also possible to maintain the idea that there is no difference between information and knowledge, by reasoning that information is simply the physical representation of knowledge or its surrogate (Farradane, 1979). However, the fact that data, information, intelligence, and knowledge involve conceptual differences is acknowledged by many authors, and a variety of definitions, from simple to complex, can be found in the literature.

Miller (2000, p. 13), an expert in CI, simply suggests that "data, when organized, becomes information; [and] information, when analyzed, becomes intelligence." Wilson (2002), a scholar of information science, defines data as simple facts and information as data embedded in context. Fuld (1995), a well-known CI consultant, describes data as scattered bits and pieces of knowledge, such as numerical data. Information is the pooling of these bits of knowledge requiring the addition of contextual meaning to data. Analysis is distilled information, and intelligence is the implication of such analysis allowing decision making. Fuld, however, does not define knowledge.

Going a step further, Choo (2002) describes information and knowledge as outcomes of human action, both resulting from a cognitive effort. An aggregation of data will bring information, and an accumulation of experience will result in knowledge. Intelligence, according to Choo, is related to the possession and creation of knowledge and characterizes an adaptive behavior. He describes an intelligent organization as one that knows how to create and use knowledge to innovate and to adapt. Thus, intelligence is related to problem solving and requires assessment and the integration of information and knowledge.

For Meadow et al. (2000, p. 35) data refers to a "string of elementary symbols, such as digits or letters," whereas information "carries the connotation of evaluated, validated, or useful data." Knowledge, on the other hand, involves "a higher degree of certainty or validity than information" and "has the characteristic of information shared and agreed upon within a community" (Meadow et al., 2000, p. 38), and intelligence is a form of information but it is also "a measure of reasoning capacity." In other words, intelligence can be seen as deriving from information through analysis, or as a certain type of information, packaged for a specific purpose.

Mitchell (2000) also defines information as data made meaningful by being put into a context, and knowledge as data made meaningful through a set of beliefs about the causal relationships between actions and their probable consequences, gained through either inference or experience. Here, knowledge differs from information in that it is predictive and can be used to guide action while information merely contributes a context to the data. For example, if the raw data is "–10 degrees," then information would be "it is –10 degrees outside," and the knowledge would be that "–10 degrees is cold and one must dress warmly." In other words, knowledge involves experience whereas information is seen as a documentation of any piece of knowledge. For example, in the business world, the letter of the name of one top executive is merely data. The data, or letter, put into context with other letters could reveal that this is a name. Knowledge of a particular industry would reveal that it is the name of a top executive who is the new incumbent for the given position of vice president (VP), and this would become critical information. However, knowledge exists at many levels. For instance, someone who is educated about the characteristics of a VP position would possess some level of knowledge on the subject because that education would provide clues about how to interact with the new incumbent. However, having that education without sufficient experience of working in an organization will not create a high level of confidence about interacting with the VP, and thus may not be very useful. On the other hand, working within an organization for years can bring a strong understanding of the organizational culture surrounding the position of VP, regardless of education, resulting in greater ability to interpret the situation. Knowledge is generated through learning, both from experience and education. It is, however, greatly enriched through experience because knowledge deepens one's beliefs about causal relationships. That is why we may argue that knowledge is ingrained and difficult to document, as opposed to information, which can be recorded and stored.

The central importance of cognitive efforts is also recognized by Taylor (1986), who suggests that data are transformed into information when relationships between various types of data are established. Relationships provide structure and, therefore, meaning. The author developed a value-added spectrum illustrating that data can be changed into information through a number of informational organizing processes (grouping, classifying, relating, formatting, signalling, displaying). Through analyzing processes (evaluating, validating, comparing, interpreting, synthesizing), information can be transmuted into informing knowledge. Judgmental processes (presenting options, advantages, disadvantages) will modify informing knowledge into productive knowledge. Productive knowledge will result in action after decision processes (choosing, bargaining, matching goals). In this approach, then, knowledge is closer to action than information. Taylor does not posit intelligence on his value-added spectrum. Indeed, there is a slight difference between information and intelligence. The latter can be seen as information with more relationships, structure, and meaning. Intelligence is close to informing knowledge as defined by Taylor because it is information that has been filtered, examined, enhanced, and analyzed.

Table 1.1 summarizes the various definitions of data, information, intelligence and knowledge, including those used to develop our conceptual framework (in the "Meaning retained" column in Table 1.1).

Table 1.1 Concepts and Meanings

Concept	Meanings	Meaning Retained
Data	String of symbols, facts, measurements, statistics Factual information Scattered bits of knowledge	Symbols, facts, statistics
Information	Organized form of data Data with context Data with relationships Piece of knowledge that can be codified and stored Physical representation of knowledge Pooling of bits of knowledge Communication or reception of knowledge Action of informing	Data with context and relationships
Intelligence	Form of information Analyzed information Implication of analysis Measure of reasoning capacity Ability to understand and to apply knowledge	Analyzed and value-added information
Knowledge	Data/information with beliefs Information with higher certainty and validity Shared information Information with experience Organized information that is internalized Condition of knowing	Internalized information, beliefs and experience

As illustrated in Table 1.1, all these terms have various meanings, which raise semantic problems. It is relatively easy to agree on the nature of data, but there are no objective criteria to distinguish information from intelligence from knowledge—this requires judgment and subjective assessment. To gain knowledge, someone must access data, information, or intelligence, but most of all he must gain experience in relation to that information and intelligence, or at least he must learn how to apply information and intelligence in a given situation. Therefore, in order to obtain information, intelligence, or knowledge, something must be added to raw data.

Figure 1.1 illustrates the approach wherein data with context equals information, information with meaning equals intelligence, and information and/or intelligence with experience generates knowledge, which is the basis for action. Instead of a continuum, the figure reflects the qualitative changes or levels involved in the transformation of the various entities, and the fuzziness of the concepts.

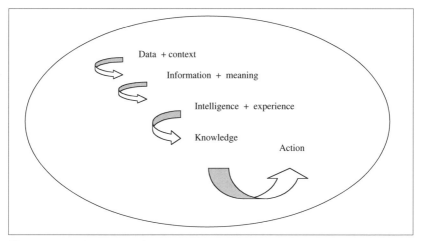

Figure 1.1 Links Between Concepts

These differentiations are well illustrated, when examining the distinct roles performed by information specialists, intelligence professionals, and experts. By selecting and organizing information resources (data with context), information specialists and librarians seek to offer a service (a library, a collection) or a system (a database) of value. However, usually their role does not consist of adding meaning to the content of these resources in a traditional sense, but rather, organizing information resources in order to facilitate the retrieval of information. These types of professionals deal with the container (a PDF or HTML document, a book, a journal, a videotape), not the content. However, by classifying disparate resources, they provide a context for those resources, which adds value and meaning to them. For example, by attaching a subject heading such as computer science to a group of publications, as opposed to, say, sociology, librarians establish structure and relationships that facilitate the retrieval of those publications and at the same time add meaning. The publication ceases to be a nondifferentiated "journal" and becomes a "journal in computer science" or a "journal in sociology."

On the other hand, experts are those who will use information and intelligence to make decisions, to make recommendations, and to take actions. Business experts have knowledge based on significant experience in a given area: strategy, finances, marketing, research and development, human resources, or production. They own an expertise allowing them to reach a higher level of interpretation of information than information professionals.

Somewhere in between information professionals and experts lies the competitive intelligence professional. CI practitioners, or analysts as they are often called, transform raw data and information into intelligence by collecting and organizing information resources, a fundamental step, but also by extracting information and adding value by assessing the relevance of the information in a particular context. The work of CI professionals involves retrieving appropriate sources of information, extracting relevant pieces of information, analyzing the information, and packaging it to offer a final product that responds to the intelligence needs of a particular decision maker or community of decision makers. They must use their judgment both to identify intelligence needs and to determine how the information acquired fulfills those intelligence needs. By applying their value judgment to information, not only to resources, analysts add more value to it.

For example, in financial circles, a beta value of 1.2 is merely data. When it is connected to the name of a stock, it becomes a piece of information. A CI professional who retrieves and presents the beta value of other stocks from a given industry for comparative purposes, would add context and meaning to the information. But to really understand the value of the information and intelligence, one must be an expert in the area of finance. Only an expert is in the position to use that intelligence, given his or her knowledge and expertise, to make recommendations about potential financial decisions. It is apparent, then, that intelligence is a mixture of data, information, and the expertise owned by the intelligence professional, which all contribute to meet the specific needs or to support specific types of decisions or reflections. In this scenario, information specialists acquire and provide access to the "information resource," competitive intelligence practitioners assign a value to its content by assessing "the information is important because …," and the expert decides what action should be taken and infers "based on my past experience and my knowledge, and in light of this information we should …"

Both in theory and in practice, the lines between information specialists, CI specialists, and experts are blurred. CI analysts often have an accumulated knowledge of various areas such as finance or marketing, thus applying their expert knowledge toward transforming information into intelligence. Likewise information specialists are

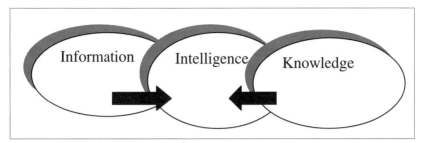

Figure 1.2   Relationships Between Basic Concepts

increasingly asked to analyze information in addition to their traditional tasks of acquiring and organizing information. Thus, the value
added to information by these various activities is often determined
by the roles assigned, but also by the knowledge base of the individual performing the activity.

Reviewing the meanings outlined in Table 1.1, we see that information is data with context and relationships, and intelligence is
information with meaning added. In other words, intelligence is
information with more relationships and meaning attached to it.
Knowledge, then, is information that has been internalized, and is
associated with beliefs and experience. Figure 1.2 is a representation
of these definitions, illustrating the idea that intelligence is at the
intersection between information and knowledge (or expertise) and
is indeed a mixture of both. To analyze information and to add value
to it, special knowledge is required. But, it is true also that access to
intelligence might generate new knowledge. A dynamic relationship
connects all of these terms, and we should remember this when considering the role of technologies for managing data, information,
intelligence, and knowledge.

The Notion of Value

Before we begin our discussion about "value-added information," it
is necessary to describe in more detail the nature of information as a
resource. Today, few would disagree with the idea that information is
a key resource in society and organizations. Many studies have shown
that the majority of the working population is involved in producing
and using information, characterizing the information economy.

Nevertheless, information is a very special kind of resource, a commodity with very particular characteristics. According to Cronin (1984), unlike crude oil and coffee beans, information cannot be "exhausted." He correctly raises the fact that certain pieces of information can become obsolete and others can have multiple life cycles. There is no restriction to the number of users of information. Many users of information will diminish neither its quantity nor its quality, and more information for one user does not mean less for another. Thus, in a way, information can be perceived as a public good.

Cleveland (1982) suggests that information is expandable because it can increase with use, as is the case for scientific information. The more we have, the more we use, and the more we increase the quantity and quality of information. But, information is also compressible, since it can be summarized or concentrated to facilitate its use. Information is also almost instantaneously transportable using various technologies, regardless of its original location (in the past by telegraph and now via the Internet). Information is diffusive, it tends to leak, and it presents a challenge for those who wish to control it. Information is shared as opposed to exchanged, because someone can give it away and still retain it at the same time. Information is substitutable because it can replace other resources, such as land or capital and, presumably, because it is an asset easily stored, requiring minimal physical facilities, and allowing financial decisions involving a minimum of capital.

All of these qualities reveal information as a unique resource. It is like money and water because it can be reused and recycled (Best, 1988). But unlike money and water, anyone can create it, and it can be used simultaneously with someone else for different purposes. Information has a dynamic dimension (as opposed to being static) in that it can take on many forms, serve many goals, have many lives, and play many roles. For Eaton and Bawden (1991), the dynamics of information contribute to the formative and organizing function of the resource. Indeed, the word information derives from the Latin "informare," which means "to give form to." The use and value of information as a resource is unpredictable and depends on many variables: the user, the environment, the situation at hand, the need for the information, and many other factors such as the availability and quality of information sources.

To summarize, the nature of information is unique in two ways: Its life cycle is peculiar and not easy to predict, and the consumption of information does not lead to less information. As a result, the value of information is not readily quantifiable. Although it is possible to measure the cost of its production, measuring its value remains a challenge.

The notion of value is central to the idea of value-added information. In this section, we want to precede our description of value-added processes with a discussion about the value of information. We all know that value is the worth of something. To say that something has value involves a comparison between two objects or two states, and the belief that one is preferable to the other. In business, people are familiar with the *market value* of resources, or what resources can be exchanged for on the market. Indeed the notion of value has been addressed in the economics literature. Adam Smith, a pioneer of economic thought, distinguishes two types of value: The *value in exchange*, or "exchange value," is the purchasing power of a resource. This concept implies an agreed-upon price between two parties, the owner of the resource and the potential buyer. The exchange value here is similar to the market value. The *value in use* is the utility of a particular resource for a specific task, or the benefit that the user obtains from the use of the resource. The notion that information has value, that it is a resource similar to other commodities, and that value can be added to it, is widely accepted in many quarters. However, as we have seen, given the unique characteristics of information, the calculation and even the demonstration of the existence of the value of information are difficult endeavours.

The predicament is that what is of value to one individual may be very different than what is of value to another, both in the type of information and the amount of value added. In a study investigating how the information needs of managers were addressed by CI analysts, Westney and Ghoshal (1994) reveal some very different viewpoints regarding the nature of value-added information. For one manager, value-added information means information that was drastically summarized; whereas for another, condensing information was extremely inappropriate and only large quantities of information were considered valuable. In addition, the researchers rightly point out that information with little value added to it (for example, the announcement that a competitor is sponsoring an event) can be very valuable in itself and result in immediate action, but some other discrete pieces of information (for example, a competitor's earnings per share ratio without explanations or analysis) will need more value added to be useful.

Outside the field of economics, the concept of value is a fundamental notion for philosophers. Long before Adam Smith, Aristotle addressed the various dimensions of value. Saracevic and Kantor (1997) summarize the four types of value that are sometimes distinguished in philosophy: Something has *intrinsic value* when it is good in itself, such as "being informed"; *extrinsic or instrumental value,* which applies to a resource or a means that supports the intrinsic value of something (for example, information supports the state of being informed); *inherent value,* which applies to an entity that contributes to the intrinsic value of something (for example, a specific well-known document or journal that might have an inherent value because of its status, and thus contribute to being informed); and *contributory value,* which exists when something contributes to the value of a whole. An information service has contributory value because it helps a number of people to be better informed. For these authors, information only has extrinsic value, since it is instrumental in supporting the state of being informed. Similarly, Eaton and Bawden (1991) and others have also argued that information has no intrinsic value, given that it depends on who is using it, and the context within which it is being used. On the other hand, some profess that information has an *imputed value,* or a value that can be anticipated (Meadow et al., 2000). Indeed, it is conceivable that one might perceive that a piece of information has future value based on one's intuition, judgment, or experience.

Given this discussion, we can see that numerous problems are associated with the value of information. Value exists in a number of ways, monetary and exchange, intrinsic or extrinsic. It is easy to suggest that information has value, but eminently difficult to demonstrate this and to define which types of value are actually attached to information. It is fair to say, however, that information has no value *per se* or no intrinsic value simply because the value of information is relative, depending on the context, the actors involved, the circumstances, or the issues at stake. In fact, Stenson et al. (2000) found in a study of U.K. companies, that the value of information is measured differently depending on the audience and purpose: For an external audience, information is assessed according to its contribution to the entire enterprise (for example, in financial reporting); and for an internal audience, information is assessed according to its contribution to the decision-making process. In the context of CI, information definitely has an instrumental and contributory value. It has instrumental value because it supports the state of being informed, the creation of intelligence. And it has contributory value because it contributes to the whole organizational decision-making process. The idea of adding value to information through the CI process suggests that not only does information have some kind of value, but also that its value can be augmented through some manipulation. The question is how can this be achieved?

As previously discussed, although information is a very special resource or commodity, its value can be expressed in terms of usefulness. This is the main argument brought forth by Taylor (1986), who stated that the value of information, for the most part, lies in its usefulness to users. In other words, information users must perceive that information will be useful before assigning any value to it. Hence, the "use value" of information is central to its nature and precedes any "exchange value" it may have. Indeed, someone is likely to pay for information only if it is perceived as useful in the first place. In pursuance of this idea, it may be argued that, in the context of CI, adding value to information means augmenting its usefulness by ensuring that it responds to the needs of users.

Is it possible to measure initial and added value? There is no one generally accepted means of measuring the value of information, which is, in fact, often confused with the value of information services or, as suggested by Yates-Mercer and Bawden (2002), "information accounting," which mainly involves the calculation of the cost of acquiring or replacing information.

The three basic approaches to measuring the value of information and information services (Ahituv and Neuman, 1986), which have contributed to the field of economics of information, have different focuses. The *normative value approach* seeks to establish the utility of information for decision making using rigorous models (e.g., statistical decision theory), for example, the value of marketing studies. Unfortunately, the studies based on that approach are not conclusive, mainly because they try to calculate the hypothetical monetary value of a document. The studies attempt to measure what people are willing to pay for information, not what its value is in the decision-making process (Repo, 1989).

The *realistic value approach* attempts to measure the impact of information by examining the effect of information on the outcomes of decision making or on performance. By comparing the situation before and after its use, the idea is to isolate information according to its key variable. Feeney and Grieves (1994) describe some of the studies undertaken from this perspective in which identifying the use value of information was central to the evaluation of information.

The *perceived value approach* examines how users perceive the value of information. In this approach, value is established by identifying the perceived benefits of information by those using it. This approach involves a subjective valuation of information by the user, which is later quantified into time or cost savings. Griffiths and King (1993), Marshall (1993), and Matarazzo and Prusak (1995) offer interesting examples of studies falling into this category. These studies assume, implicitly or explicitly, that the value of information is close to or similar to the value of information services and libraries. Indeed, information, or the output of services such as reference services, online catalogues, or current awareness services, is difficult to assess without inference to the service itself. These approaches express a basic dilemma: Is it possible to establish the value of information objectively or is it purely a subjective endeavour?

In the field of information science, the subjective aspect of value as it relates to information services has garnered the interest of many researchers. One recent discussion in this area was undertaken by Saracevic and Kantor (1997), who developed a taxonomy of value for using information services involving 90 categories or dimensions. Their taxonomy suggests that value has three main facets: the reasons for using such services, the interaction with the services or the qualities of the various aspects of services, and the results (e.g., cognitive, affective, time, and money). As we can see, the notion of value is not only complex but also multidimensional because it encompasses the multiple perceptions of users. Beyond their differences and difficulties, one thing is common to all of these approaches. They all make the assumption that using information generates some form of benefit and improvement to performance or productivity.

From a more practical point of view, information use can be viewed as beneficial for at least one of four reasons. It can help to reduce costs, to improve decision making, to save time, and to yield higher customer satisfaction (Volpe National Transportation Systems Center, U.S. Department of Transportation, 1998). Attempts to quantify these benefits invariably rely on the real or hypothetical perceptions of the users of information. Again, we find the problem that the perceived value of information is interconnected with the value of its accompanying services and technologies. Indeed, it is difficult to distinguish the value of information from the value of the services and technologies that support the delivery of the information.

Avoiding any reference to perceptions, Liautaud (2001) proposes a formula to measure the value of a given piece of information. Value increases with the square of the number of users who can access it, multiplied by the number of business areas in which they work. For example, if 10 employees in the sales department have access to a piece of information, the value would be 100 (or 10^2 x 1). However, if 10 employees from two different departments (for instance, five from Sales and five from Marketing) have access to the information, the value would be 200 (or 10^2 x 2). Although this approach is interesting, it does not really measure the value of information, but offers a formula for calculating the potential synergy of information resulting from a larger distribution of the resource.

In the management field, the value of information has been simply defined as the difference between the payoff from a decision made without information and the one from a decision made with information (Huber, 1980). This approach could potentially place a tremendous value on information, if it is seen to have contributed to, for instance, successful strategic planning or avoiding bankruptcy. However, the contribution of information to decision making is also very subjective.

The attempts to quantify and qualify the value of information are interesting and useful, but ultimately do not help to explain what is meant by "value-added information." How can we add value to a resource that more often than not has no monetary value? Also, given the multiple life cycles of information, both its retrospective and its future value are difficult to measure with precision, even from the perspective of users. This explains why the value of information services and systems is more often targeted for measurement rather than information per se.

About the functions of libraries, Atkinson (1996) wrote that the purpose of information services is to add value to certain sources of information from the perspective of users. Consequently, the main function of these types of services is to add access value to objects of information in order to reduce access time to a subset of objects. Similarly, an information system is intended to reduce access time to a particular subset of information resources that has been selected on the basis of its content value. This focus on access time has led to the "disintermediation" of information services, or the development of mechanical links empowering users to access resources without the direct assistance of human mediation. For example, more and more libraries are now offering online access to their catalogues and online reference services. Many information technology products that reduce the need for human intermediaries are designed, in principle, to decrease access time for the end-users thereby adding some type of value automatically. Thus, the value of information is linked to the systems and services attached to it. Information, having no intrinsic value in itself, must be used to have value. The value of information is also tied to the user's ability to access it and thus can be measured in part on the basis of the values added to information through a number of services and processes. Because information and value are difficult concepts to define from an operational point of view, it is necessary to see how the treatment of information positively affects its value and what type of value is actually added and how. The value-added model described in the next section offers this type of approach.

The Value-Added Processes of Information Systems

Information services and systems are the mechanisms used for delivering, storing, organizing, and packaging information. Services involve certain types of human interaction, and systems involve certain types of human-computer interaction. Both are very costly to develop and maintain, and their existence is mainly justified by the assumption that users will use them in order to extract some kind of value. As we have seen in the previous section, the concept of value as it applies to information is very broad, ill defined, and difficult to measure from the perspective of the information user. Another way to approach the valuation of information-related activities is to consider information services and systems as a series of value-added processes "by which the potential usefulness of specific input messages being processed is enhanced" (Taylor, 1986, p. 6). Here, value is added when the information is made more useful to the users by enabling them to make decisions or to clarify problems. For example, the usefulness of information is confirmed when someone selects a particular piece of information from among other pieces of information. Such a selection might be made based on the information being more meaningful, more appealing, or more relevant to the user. There may be other reasons for selection, such as the information was more conveniently available, some parts of the information were highlighted, or the information was easier to retrieve. In other words, information must go through some value-added processes in order to be noticed and selected. An information service or system, then, is useful and efficient if it properly helps the user to identify potentials, to select information, and to make better decisions. Therefore, value-added processes, according to Taylor, are those activities performed by information services and systems that offer *the means* to both signal the potential of information and to relate it to specific problems in specific environments.

Different systems may add different types of value to information. Ideally, a system should be designed for a specific *information use environment*. This expression, coined by Taylor, refers to the idea that information is always used in a specific context for specific reasons and the technology for managing information should be adapted to address the particular needs of such an environment. Although information is often used in business for decision making, this is an example of just one type of information use environment.

Based on a review of the literature, Taylor identifies six broad categories of criteria that users employ to select systems and services: *ease of use, noise reduction, quality, adaptability, time savings,* and *cost savings.* These criteria, which encompass 23 types of values that an information system can add, are described in the following pages. Interestingly, the author labelled these values as *interface*, which is the negotiating space between the system and the user. It suggests that values are indeed perceived in such a negotiating space. Having defined the values that can be added, Taylor lists examples of value-added processes achieved by a system or a service. Although the values can also apply to information services involving human interaction, we have reviewed them here in the context of computer-based information systems in order to appreciate the relevance of Taylor's framework for examining new information technologies.

Ease of use corresponds to the various elements of a system that reduce its difficulty to use. It encompasses a number of dimensions: browsing, or the capability of scanning the information neighborhood; formatting, or the possibility of arranging data/information for efficient scanning and selection; interfacing, which refers to the capacity of the system to assist users through providing answers to users' questions (mediation) and educating them about the potential uses of a system (orientation); ordering, which refers to displaying information in an orderly fashion by grouping and structuring search results; and, finally, physical access, or the ease with which users can gain access to the information entities (e.g., documents or publications). The *ease of use* dimensions just described are performed through a number of processes, such as alphabetizing information entities or highlighting important items.

Noise reduction is performed through the elimination of unwanted information (exclusion), the retention of information that has potential value (inclusion), and precision (ensuring that only precisely defined information is retrieved). This category involves the following values: intellectual access, linkage, precision, and selectivity. Intellectual access is achieved by attaching nametags, subject descriptions, and subject summaries to each information entity, enabling users to select and narrow down the set of useful information. These features give information about the content of information entities and facilitate access. Linkage, on the other hand, supposes connections between entities by setting up pointers, which should increase users' options by directing them toward other entities. Precision helps users find exactly what they look for by providing signals on information attributes and by ranking searching outputs. Selectivity is value added when the system is capable of selecting certain information chunks that meet the user requirements or needs before these chunks are allowed into the system. Therefore, selectivity occurs at the input side, as opposed to precision, which takes place at the output side. The processes that reduce noise are indexing, vocabulary control, and filtering.

Quality has to do with the excellence of the system. Accuracy is the first value that ensures quality and refers to the error-free transmission of information. Comprehensiveness is achieved when the coverage of a topic or subject is complete in relation to specific user needs, situations, and problems. Currency is the capability of the system to retrieve the most recent information and also to update the signals that are necessary to retrieve information (descriptors or nametags). Reliability implies consistency in the system performance or its capacity to maintain a certain level of quality. Validity suggests some mechanisms for signalling the soundness of the retrieved information. These values reveal the various facets of quality that are achieved through several processes such as quality control, editing, updating, analyzing, and comparing results.

The criterion *adaptability* expresses the responsiveness of the system. The values that are added in this category are closeness to problem, or the ability to respond to specific user needs or problems; flexibility, or whether the system allows several approaches for retrieving information in a dynamic way; simplicity, or when instructions and explanations are easy to grasp; and stimulatory, a value relating, for example, to the capacity of a system to encourage its use. Capabilities for manipulating retrieved information sets and searching outputs are the main processes supporting these values.

The two final user criteria, *time savings* and *cost savings*, deal with perceived values of a system in terms of response speed and money saved by users. Processes such as reducing processing time and lowering costs connected to the system are central to its value.

This framework of value-added processes is interesting because, although it is system-oriented, it is also user-centered in that it relates user criteria, and indirectly user perceptions, to the values that can be added by a system. These values express well the nature of the usefulness of an information system, in particular, with respect to the ability of a system to facilitate information retrieval.

The need to improve information systems is a long-standing concern in information science. This need often arises out of Mooers' Law, defined in 1959, which states that "an information retrieval system will tend not to be used whenever it is more painful and troublesome for a customer to have information than for him not to have it" (Mooers, 1960, p. 1). This law supports the idea that if a system is easy to use, the information contained in it is more likely to be used. Unfortunately, this has not been the corollary of the law (Austin, 2001). Mooers actually lamented the fact that accessing information is painful and troublesome, because reading it, understanding it, and thinking about it can be the source of more frustrations than not having information at all. This is the basis for his argument that some people might not want information. In the end, the real factor determining the use of an information system is not its ease of use or its usefulness, but rather the context in which its use takes place, and whether or not the use of information is valued in a particular environment. Thus, the determinant factor is the information culture. If the use of information is rewarded, an information system will be used even though it may be poorly designed. There is, then, no need for a discussion about the value of an information system or service unless the information-use environment places a value on information in the first place.

The Value-Added Processes of Expert and Intelligent Systems

In the field of artificial intelligence, the major preoccupation is with developing expert systems. An expert system is a software program designed to simulate the problem-solving behavior of a human who is an expert in a narrow domain or discipline. Such systems are typically composed of a knowledge base (information, heuristics, etc.), inference engine (analyzes the knowledge base), and the end-user interface (accepting inputs, generating outputs). As discussed earlier, experts use their knowledge to assess information and make decisions. The value added to information using an expert system is different in kind than the value added by information systems. An expert system is useful for making recommendations, routine decisions, or decisions that are relatively easy to program following pre-established patterns (e.g., "if this happens, then this should be done"). The value of an expert system is its ability to transform information into decision making through a built in "inference mechanism." Thus the value added to information by an expert system is similar to the one added by an expert who infers action from information based on pre-existing knowledge and experience in a particular subject area.

Somewhere in between an expert system and an information system falls the intelligence system, as represented by competitive intelligence systems. Although CI software does add the same kind of value to information as that added by an information system (such as Taylor's 23 dimensions), ideally it should also have some characteristics of an expert system in order to represent an intelligent system. Basic to the concept of CI is the process of analysis. And, at one level, it can be said that information systems do provide some level of analysis by indexing, filtering, and comparing results. These processes are considered by many to contribute significantly to the function of analysis. However, as illustrated in Figure 1.1, intelligence is created by attaching a higher level of meaning to information than can be performed by an information system. Traditionally, the output of a CI system, whether human-based or technology-based, is not "decision making" per se but rather advice, hypothesis, and forecasts that can be used by decision makers. A CI system should process information to a state in which the meaning of that information is weighed and understood. Such a system does not necessarily require a highly specialized knowledge base, but should incorporate information about a given industry and its competitive conditions in order to help the user of such a system recognize threats and opportunities. A CI system should assist a user in becoming aware of relationships between various types of information in order to reach some conclusions. Hence, the values added to information by a CI system are different in nature than those added by a basic information system within which information is simply deposited and manipulated. On the other hand, the development of an expert system for CI seems rather improbable, as CI-related decisions require the consideration of a large body of information and exist in a highly unstable and rapidly changing external environment, with few pre-established patterns.

In conclusion, the idea that information has value is implicit in today's economy. But measuring the value of information presents insurmountable challenges because of its special characteristics. The purpose of information-related systems is to add or increase the value of information. There are a number of ways of adding value to information. At the first level, value can be added through basic information processes, such as alphabetizing, indexing, filtering, and comparing. At the second level, value can be added through applying context and meaning to information, transforming it into intelligence. The closer an information-related system is situated to the decision-making process, the greater the amount of value that must be added to the information, and the greater the number of value-adding processes. CI, whether conducted by humans or mediated by a CI system, is a business function that requires value to be added at both of these levels. In the next chapter, we discuss the concept of CI and present the value-added processes involved with CI in detail.

CHAPTER 2

A Conceptual Framework for Competitive Intelligence

Competitive intelligence is a hot topic in the business world today. CI training courses, workshops, seminars, and books abound and membership levels in CI-related associations have been climbing steadily since the 1980s. CI has been reported as one of the fastest growing disciplines in the U.S. (SCIP, 2002; Miller, 2000; Kahaner, 1998). Despite its rising popularity, or perhaps as a result of it, CI suffers from some of the characteristics that are common to many new methodologies and disciplines. To begin with, the concept of CI is very vague. Numerous definitions of CI available in the literature are imprecise and inclusive, and the expression is often used interchangeably with other related concepts, such as business intelligence and competitor analysis. Second, there are only a few conceptual models, and they are not particularly helpful for gaining a comprehensive understanding of CI. The need for a more systematic approach to CI has been raised by Hall (2001), who conducted a survey of Australian managers and discovered that they used very basic sources for gaining competitive information (rumors, newspapers) due to a lack of knowledge regarding CI techniques and sources.

The purpose of this chapter is to discuss the various definitions of CI found in the literature in order to more precisely describe its nature, beginning with a brief discussion of the historical background of CI and its recent rise in popularity in North America. Next, we examine the various definitions of CI, outlining its existing ambiguities and overlaps with related concepts. Following this, we discuss the theoretical roots of CI, tracing its evolution to its current state of practice, and examine its relationship with other management functions. Finally, we present our information-processing model of CI, discuss how this model relates to some of the other models, and outline in detail each step contained in the CI cycle.

The Evolution of Competitive Intelligence

The techniques of intelligence have evolved over the course of human history and the traditions of spying and of surveying the environment go back thousands of years. Sun Tzu's classic work *The Art of War*, a masterpiece on military strategies, may represent the origin of CI practice (Fleisher and Blenkhorn, 2001). It was more than 2,000 years ago that Sun Tzu argued that one will not be in danger in a hundred battles if one knows his enemy and himself. This basic premise remains alive and well today, as competing in the business arena without knowing one's competitors has been likened to playing a game in the dark (McGonagle and Vella, 1999). The term "intelligence" has long been used in military operations to represent gathering secrets from the enemy. However, CI as a systematized and conceptualized activity is much more recent, especially so in North America. In some other parts of the world, such as Asia and Europe, companies have been employing advanced CI systems for much longer.

Culture plays a large role in the practices of CI in various countries. Kahaner (1998) conducted a study that examined the CI practices in various countries, and offers the only work describing in such detail the cultural differences in CI. The Japanese, who are said to have an "absolute and unbending" belief in CI, conduct it in partnership with other companies, organizations, and government departments working toward the common goal of increasing the competitiveness of the entire country. The Japanese government, which has always played a supportive role in industry, has a strong research function in the Japanese economy and provides Japanese companies with analysis of their industries, markets, and competitors through their Ministry of Finance, Trade and Culture; the Japan External Trade Organization; and the Japanese embassies. The Japan External Trade Organization, which is now mandated to assist foreigners conducting business in Japan, was originally founded in 1951 to provide research about the competition to Japanese businesses operating in foreign markets. Although North American companies have traditionally focused their external scanning on customer-related information, the Japanese have long recognized the value of scanning the external environment for competitor information. The Japanese approach to CI tends to focus on the collection and synthesis of large amounts of information about competitors.

A serious interest and investment in CI extends beyond Japan to most other parts of Asia, including countries such as South Korea, Thailand, Singapore, and even China (Tao and Prescott, 2000), where intense market competition exacerbates the need for adapted and new intelligence practices.

European companies, on the other hand, are generally thought to place a stronger emphasis on the analytical aspect of CI, relying more heavily on intuition and experience than the Japanese (Kahaner, 1998). The European approach, best exemplified in the United Kingdom, Germany, Sweden, and Denmark, echoes CI practices in Japan, in that companies and government institutions work together to gather and exchange information about foreign competitors for the good of the national economy. Governments play a critical role in fostering the development of CI practices. Most countries in Europe have a long history of government involvement in providing intelligence for their national firms. For example, in 1971 a group of Swedish banks cooperated to form their own CI research organization to provide information about their competitors in foreign markets. And, in Germany, the Bayer Corporation is well known for systematically analyzing the patents of its competitors as early as 1886.

Even though numerous examples of these types of interrelationships can be found in both Europe and Asia, the notion of companies sharing information with each other or in collusion with governmental organizations for the good of the nation flies in the face of American culture. The free-market approach to industry in the U.S., which admonishes government intervention into business, has greatly influenced the nature of CI within the U.S. and, indeed, throughout North America. Programs and partnerships between governments and industry are much less common, as is the practice of sharing information with other companies. Kahaner (1998) suggests that, as a result of this cultural climate, CI has not flourished as much as it has in other parts of the world. Few North American firms practiced any form of CI before the 1980s, and those that did, such as GE, did so mainly in an informal, unstructured way. Choo (2002) also notes that corporations in the U.S. are behind Japanese organizations in the area of environmental scanning and business intelligence.

Since the 1980s, however, the popularity of CI in North America has been on the rise. The results of a survey conducted by the U.S.

Conference Board in 1988 reflect this. Of the more than 300 U.S. marketing, sales, and planning managers who responded to the survey, 68 percent indicated that monitoring competitors' activities was "very important" and 30 percent indicated that it was "fairly important" (Sutton, 1988). The growth in the membership of the Society of Competitive Intelligence Professionals (SCIP) since its inception in 1986 also reflects the rise in interest in formalized CI since the mid-1980s. Initially launched with a few regional chapters in the U.S., SCIP now boasts 60 chapters in more than 20 countries, as publicized on its Web site. Showing a similar trend, CI conferences and publications also increased dramatically in the 1990s (Fleisher and Blenkhorn, 2001).

A number of factors have contributed to the recent growth in CI as a management function in North America. In particular, globalization has greatly enhanced the competitiveness of markets. Competitive conditions are changing constantly and at no time in the past have there been so many opportunities or dangers for businesses, both large and small. In the 1970s and '80s, U.S. industries experienced some huge losses as a result of globalization, in combination with a laissez-faire attitude toward new competitors. The prime example of this is the oft-told story of the U.S. automobile industry. American manufacturers lost substantial market share to Japanese manufacturers by failing to foresee the popularity of more fuel-efficient automobiles. In most industries today, enterprises must compete with other businesses around the world. Not only must companies be more inclusive in the number of competitors being monitored, but they must learn to understand the behavior of companies from other cultures. Gaining an understanding of the strategic behavior of unfamiliar competitors from outside one's borders presents a far greater challenge than understanding long-established competitors from the same culture. Given these conditions, CI has become recognized as an increasingly critical activity.

New technology has also contributed to an increase in CI activities (Rouach and Santi, 2001; Gates, 1999). It is now easy for companies to access up-to-the-minute news, financial information, and other details required for CI through information databases and company Web sites via the Internet, making the job of information retrieval more efficient than in the past. Most CI specialists now believe that virtually all information required for CI is readily and legally available to those who know how to find it (Fleisher and Blenkhorn, 2001).

Finally, the rise of CI has accompanied the growing popularity of two other interrelated management functions: marketing and strategic planning. As a subfield of marketing, marketing intelligence (Kelley, 1965) emerged as a distinct discipline several decades ago and contributed to the establishment of some intellectual foundations of CI. The analysis of market trends, of consumer behavior, and of marketing strategies are key when conducting CI. Following the seminal work of Kelley, Michael E. Porter laid down more foundations for CI. Competitor intelligence (or, synonymously, competitor analysis) was coined in the 1980s by Porter and gained widespread recognition through his book, *Competitive Strategy: Techniques for Analyzing Industries and Competitors*. His model involves four diagnostic components: future goals, current strategy, assumptions, and capabilities. Analyzing these four components of one's competitors will allow a company to develop a competitor response profile in order to predict how they will behave in the future, and hence plan an effective strategy (Porter, 1980). The expression "competitive intelligence" began to appear as managers adapted Porter's CI model to the specific needs of their company and industry.

The rise of strategic planning began in the 1950s. The function achieved prominence in management circles from the mid-1960s through the mid-1970s, during which time many business people viewed it as the answer to all their management problems. It seemed to drop out of sight for the next decade or so, enjoying a revival in the 1990s (Mintzberg, 1994). The more recent approaches to strategy involve the positioning of a business to maximize the value of its capabilities in order to distinguish it from its competitors. Clearly, CI has a strategic role, and corporate strategic plans cannot be fully developed without a good grasp of the trends in a given industry and the activities of one's competitors. CI is now considered an essential part of any corporate system aimed at providing strategic information.

Defining Competitive Intelligence

Despite the rapid proliferation of the CI function in North America, it is rarely defined in a comprehensive way. This may be a reflection of the relative infancy of the concept. The literature is full of vague statements about how CI will increase competitiveness, as well as declarations about how it is an ethical and legal activity, and not industrial espionage. Of some concern is the fact that much of the CI literature has been written by those with a stake in its growth, thus placing a greater emphasis on promoting the function than on providing useful insights into the concept and its practical application. Confusing the issue even more is the fact that many in the business community use the terms "competitor analysis," "competitive intelligence," and "business intelligence" interchangeably.

Practitioners and theorists have largely failed to agree on a common definition of CI. Although consensus about some aspects of the function has been achieved, a review of some of the more commonly found definitions provides insight into where the obscurities lie:

- Fuld & Co. a high-profile CI consulting firm, takes an inclusive approach in defining the function of CI:

  "Competitive intelligence can mean many things to many people. A research scientist sees it as a heads-up on a competitor's new R&D initiatives. A salesperson considers it insight on how his or her company should bid against another firm in order to win a contract. A senior manager believes intelligence to be a long-term view on a marketplace and its rivals" (Fuld & Co. Web site, 2002).

- The Society for Competitive Intelligence Professionals (SCIP), the most active CI association in North America, is a little more precise:

  "A systematic and ethical program for gathering, analyzing, and managing external information that can affect your company's plans, decisions, and operations. Put another way, CI is the process of enhancing marketplace competitiveness through a greater—yet unequivocally ethical—understanding of a firm's competitors and the competitive environment" (SCIP Web site, 2002).

- Miller (2000, p. 13) argues that "intelligence is more than reading newspaper articles; it is about developing unique insights regarding issues within a firm's business environment."

- Kahaner (1998, p. 16) offers this definition:

  "Competitive intelligence is a systematic program for gathering and analyzing information about your competitors' activities and general business trends to further your own company's goals."

- And, finally, this definition from John E. Prescott, a professor of business administration at the University of Pittsburgh:

  "A formalized, yet continuously evolving process by which the team assesses the evolution of its industry and the capabilities and behavior of its current and potential competitors to assist in maintaining or developing a competitive advantage" (Prescott and Gibbons, cited in Malhotra, 1996).

A recent review of terminology and definitions relating to CI (Bergeron and Hiller, 2002) concludes that although the concept of CI is indeed fuzzy, the term has nevertheless been preferred by SCIP over a similar concept, "competitor intelligence," which was in use for a number of years (Barndt, 2000). To begin our discussion, we can see that, although the definitions imply vague conceptual differences, they do have a number of things in common. First of all, it is generally agreed that CI is an information-gathering process or activity. Second, the focus of CI is on the external environment and includes a company's competitors (rivals). Third, there is a consensus that the purpose of CI is to increase, or maintain, a company's competitiveness. And finally, the use of the terms "insight," "understanding," "analysis," and "assess" indicates that some type of analysis is practiced through CI. To summarize the commonalities, CI is defined as an information-gathering process involving the analysis of a company's external environment, including its competitors, in order to remain competitive.

Table 2.1 Scope of CI

Author	Scope of CI
Fuld & Co.	A *marketplace* and its rivals.
SCIP	A firm's competitors and the *competitive environment*.
Miller	A firm's business environment.
Kahaner	Competitors' activities and *general business trends*.
Prescott & Gibbons	An *industry* and the capabilities and behavior of its current and potential competitors.

The confusion occurs when we look at the nature of the external environment as described in each of these definitions. We will call this the "scope" of the CI function. All five definitions agree that competitors are included in such a scope, but each definition also makes a vague reference to other factors that should be included in the analysis. Table 2.1 shows the different approaches to defining the scope of the "competitive intelligence" environment in the previously given definitions.

These definitions imply that CI includes other factors beyond the analysis of competitors. The definitions, which describe the environment as a marketplace, a competitive environment, general business trends, and an industry, provide little guidance to the practitioner as to what other factors (e.g., sales, relationships with suppliers, government subsidies) are relevant and important when performing competitive intelligence.

What factors should be included in the scope of CI? To gain a better understanding of this, it is helpful to distinguish CI from several related terms. The concepts of competitor intelligence, business intelligence, market intelligence, and competitive intelligence are often used interchangeably in the business community. The fact is that all of these activities involve analysis of the external environment, but each activity differs slightly in its purpose and information requirements. The scope of competitor intelligence, as defined by Porter, is fairly clear-cut and includes five forces: existing competitors, threats of new entrants, threats of substitute products, bargaining power of suppliers, and bargaining power of buyers. These five groups of actors constitute the focus of Porter's Five Forces Model. Porter also defined what components, or variables, should be diagnosed when conducting competitive analysis: future goals, current strategy, assumptions, and capabilities of competitors and competitors' response profiles.

CI, on the other hand, is broader in scope. In addition to competitors, the scope of the environment includes other aspects that affect the competitiveness of a company, such as government subsidies, economic policies, mergers and acquisitions, and even demographics and political context. Although competitor intelligence is a subset of CI, the latter might include data about noncompetitors that might be instrumental in gaining an additional competitive edge for a company.

If we look at CI practices, Porter's Five Forces Model is considered to be one of many types of analytical techniques that can be used by CI practitioners to understand where they have a competitive advantage over their competitors and where they do not. Other types of analytical techniques used in competitive intelligence (some have counted over 100 types of analysis) have different information requirements than Porter's Five Forces Model. What distinguishes CI from competitor analysis is its use of a variety of analytical techniques to understand competitor behavior. However, it is not the type of analysis that defines the scope of CI, but rather its purpose. For example, one of the most popular types of analysis in CI is the SWOT technique (strengths, weaknesses, opportunities, and threats). This technique can be performed on competitors, but also customers. Similarly, benchmarking, which is often used to discover the basic norms applied in practice in a given industry, can be used to compare competitors, customers, or one's own enterprise against a "best practice" organization.

Market intelligence or marketing intelligence (MI), on the other hand, mainly involves the analysis of a company's customers, or potential customers, and sales patterns (Rouach and Santi, 2001). It might provide insights on competitors, but most often deals with short-term and operational goals (McGonagle and Vella, 1996). MI provides tactical information, whereas CI is used to guide strategic decision making in order to obtain a competitive advantage. CI is specifically attuned to gaining insight into competitors in order to understand their behavior, predict future actions, and ultimately out-maneuver them.

Business intelligence (BI) is a broader and more inclusive concept than competitor intelligence, CI, or market intelligence. Few authors have attempted to draw a clear distinction between CI and business intelligence. A review of the literature reveals that business intelligence includes activities such as data mining, market analysis, sales analysis, and analysis of customer and supplier records and behavioral patterns, as well as CI (Liautaud, 2001). One definition of BI describes it as the activity of monitoring the environment external to the firm for information that is relevant for the decision-making process in the company (Gilad and Gilad, 1988). Another definition of BI describes it as broader than CI, including the analysis of mergers and acquisitions, risk assessments, and counter intelligence, as well as competitive intelligence (Sutton, 1988; Choo, 2002). Most often, business intelligence is used as a catch-all phrase—a category including all types of external and internal analysis conducted for an organization. In some countries such as Sweden and Denmark, however, CI and business intelligence are used synonymously (Dedijer, 1998). As shown in Figure 2.1, MI, CI, and competitor analysis are all considered to play a role in business intelligence.

Although the scope of CI does not have clearly defined boundaries, it is mainly concerned with those aspects of the external environment that help to differentiate one competitor from another. For example, government regulations would only be considered if one competitor was subject to those regulations, and another was not. Industry conditions and issues affecting all competitors, such as the regulations applied to the aerospace industry, do not influence significantly their ability to compete with each other and therefore are less crucial to monitor for CI purposes. Thus, CI is the process of analyzing those aspects of the competitive environment that contribute to distinguishing one competitor from another in order for a company to remain competitive or to increase its competitiveness. And it is a process that generates CI products, various intelligence reports, summaries, and analyses to substantiate strategic decisions.

One very important activity in CI is identifying exactly who one's competitors are. In a closed competitive environment, distinguishing one's competitors is a relatively simple process involving identifying

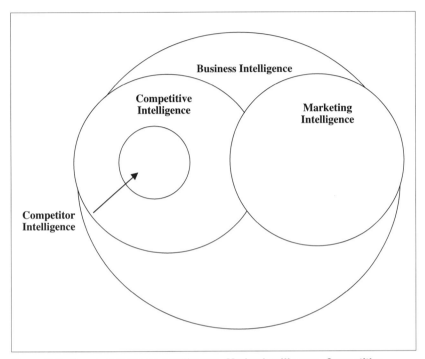

Figure 2.1   Scope of Business Intelligence, Market Intelligence, Competitive Intelligence, and Competitor Intelligence

the few companies from the same geographical region that produce similar products. However, in reality, the process is significantly more complex. Industries converge and overlap, and the once clear distinctions between product groups are becoming blurred. Although there are advantages to using narrow criteria for identifying one's competitors (it greatly simplifies the competitive intelligence process), the disadvantages are considerable. Firms can be left vulnerable to unanticipated changes in the environment resulting in severe loss of market share. Returning to our example of the U.S. automotive industry in the late 1970s, we can see the danger of defining the competitive arena too narrowly. U.S. manufacturers were highly aware of the moves of their U.S. competitors but failed to include their international counterparts in their analysis of the competitive environment, with disastrous results.

In theory, there are two traditional ways of identifying competitors: through industry-defined arenas, which identify competitors as those organizations that compete with each other when they share similar technological attributes and can produce similar products, and through market-defined arenas, which identify competitors as those organizations with output attributes that fulfill similar client functions and are thus substitutable. In practice, studies have shown that managers perceive competitors on the basis of much narrower characteristics than these theoretical boundaries, such as similar size, location, labor, capital asset structure, and so forth. In one study (Porac and Thomas, 1990), when asked to identify their competitors, Scottish knitwear producers typically cited other Scottish firms, despite the fact that the Scottish firms made up only 3 percent of worldwide production of knitwear. Likewise, other studies have found that decision makers often ignore competition from companies producing substitute products, despite the fact that the growth rate of one company has a negative influence on the growth rate of another. The study of Scottish knitwear producers illustrates this well. The surveyed manufacturers overwhelmingly identified their competitors as manufacturers of cashmere pullover sweaters. This narrow view of the competition is misguided because the surveyed producers also compete with manufacturers of garments made from fabrics such as wool, goose down, polar fleece, and Goretex. One of the potential dangers of defining one's competitors too narrowly includes loss of market share to producers of replacement products.

Porter outlined three types of competitors in his theory of competitive strategy: existing competitors, potential competitors, and companies producing substitute products. This broad approach continues to be popular in theory because it includes all the players that affect the intensity of competition. On the other hand, in practice, CI often focuses on a few major direct competitors. Conducting CI using a more inclusive approach involves time-consuming information gathering and complex analysis, which can result in intelligence that takes so long to produce that competitive conditions change, rendering the intelligence irrelevant. Company managers should keep in mind that the globalization of many markets and the rapid development of new technologies have multiplied the risks associated with defining the competitive environment too narrowly (Day, Reibstein, and Gunther, 1997). As we will see in the next section, the way the competitive environment is defined is strongly related to organizational strategy and how a company defines its market.

Rouach and Santi (2001) provide corporate examples of various CI attitudes involving different states of mind and approaches for collecting information related to a company's overall strategy. Nestlé in Switzerland is a good example. An organization that focused mainly on infant nutrition for more than a century, Nestlé has recently reinvented itself as a multinational food company. Its strategy required constant technical innovation and the launch of many new products each year as well as redefining its competition in relation to its strategy to include a much broader array of companies.

Competitive Intelligence and Strategy

Another aspect involved in identifying the competitive environment is choosing which competitor qualities are important for analysis. Should competitors be analyzed based on their financial statements, their production processes, the characteristics of their products, or something else? Indeed, there are hundreds of competitor characteristics that may potentially be considered in competitive intelligence. The aspects of a competitor that are relevant to competitive intelligence will largely depend on the purpose of the CI function within the organization.

The traditional function of CI has been to explain and predict competitor behavior in order to guide strategy. Having evolved out of Porter's conceptual model of competitor intelligence, in which "competitive strategy involves the positioning of a business to maximize the value of the capabilities that distinguish it from its competitors" (Porter, 1980), CI is often forward-looking, providing corporate strategic planners with potential response scenarios of competitors to various strategic options. The newer models of strategic planning emphasize adaptability and the importance of making decisions that will ensure the organization's ability to successfully respond to changes in the environment, rather than other types of planning, such as long-range planning, which are based on the assumption that knowledge about current conditions is sufficiently reliable to ensure the plan's viability over the duration of its implementation (Mintzberg, 1994). An organization's ability to succeed has more to do with its ability to transform itself continuously, than whether it has the right strategy. Strategic planning requires detailed information and assessment of both the internal and external environments of an organization. In theory, CI is thought to be central to planning effective strategy (Ghoshal and Westney, 1991).

Despite the theoretical connection between CI and strategic planning, studies have shown that they are not always related in practice (Fleisher and Blenkhorn, 2001). A number of studies have found that managers differ enormously in their perceptions of CI, and these differences are often related to their organizational function (Pirttilä, 1998). A study of the Finnish forest industry found that CI was disseminated and used widely throughout the organizational structure. The location of the CI department is often indicative of the purpose of such a function within an organization, and has a large influence on which competitor dimensions are addressed. For example, a CI unit that is located within a marketing department may be interested in competitors' relationships with customers, whereas one located in the R&D department may be more interested in the product designs and development processes of various competitors. Recently, SCIP reported that, "a general operating assumption [in the field of competitive intelligence] is that … top-level strategic intelligence has value" (SCIP, 2002). However, the results of a SCIP survey of CI practices conducted in 2000 indicates that there are a wide variety of locations for CI units within corporate structures. The top two departments that house CI functions are the marketing research department (46 percent) and the sales department (14 percent). These findings are inconsistent with what is prescribed in the literature. In theory, CI is directly related to strategic planning, but in practice, CI is functioning within a variety of organizational departments.

That being said, it seems there is a growing number of cases in which implementation of CI is geared to support strategic planning. At IBM in the early 1990s, CI was for the most part isolated within various business units, such as marketing, product development, and finance. These management units operated as separate entities, rarely sharing information with each other. As IBM's market share began to decline, the company set out to revise its approach to CI. By early 1995, it had greatly expanded its CI operations. Each senior executive was assigned to be the resident "expert," responsible for ensuring that strategies throughout IBM addressed its competitors and led to appropriate actions in the marketplace. To link CI with strategy, the Corporate Strategy department began to lead the program by providing a framework, a methodology, and tools to each of the virtual intelligence teams, keeping competitive intelligence visible to executives while they were developing strategies. By linking a wide range of resources and catering the CI for executives, IBM has become more proactive in the marketplace and more effective in competitive situations (Prescott and Miller, 1999). Likewise, Proctor and Gamble recently embedded its CI function within its strategy department. According to the former chairman, the CI function evolved from performing routine report generation to a pertinent activity in strategy development leading to a more robust and viable strategy (Miller, 1999).

Even in a support function for strategy, the type of analytical outcomes produced in CI can be quite varied. In the Five Forces Model of competitor analysis, Porter identifies several diagnostic components of one's competitors: future goals, current strategy, assumptions, and capabilities. Similarly, in a SWOT analysis, a competitor's strengths, weaknesses, opportunities, and threats are the dimensions required.

In order to have an effective CI function, it is important to begin with a clear idea of the purpose of CI within the firm and an understanding of those within the organization who will be its consumers. The fact that CI represents a high level of analysis highlights the need to develop CI practices on the basis of the intelligence needs of those internal consumers.

The Competitive Intelligence Process

In recent years, the awareness of process management's role for performance improvement has increased noticeably in private and public organizations (Rummler and Brache, 1995). Conventional methods of studying organizations through their vertical or functional structures were seen as inadequate for identifying vital information needed to support strategy. In contrast, process management reveals how various organizational functions operate within a system. This horizontal systems approach, based on the actual flow of materials and information, allows one to more easily identify what is being produced, who the customers are, how work gets done, and how the different functions are involved in the various process stages (Dervitsiotis, 1999). Process management, which was originally developed to evaluate manufacturing processes, has more recently been applied to other organizational processes such as information flow and communication networks. Traditional models of managing information systems place a large emphasis on technology, or are

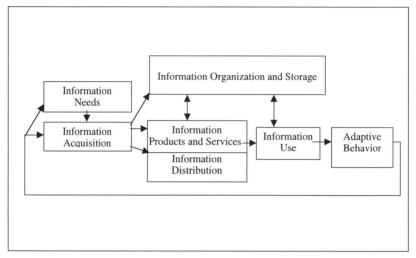

Figure 2.2   Information Management Cycle (adapted from Choo, 2002)

based on economic models. These were considered sufficient when information was thought to play merely a support role in organizational performance. However, as industries move toward knowledge-based resources and services, the effectiveness of information and intelligence systems is increasingly tied to organizational outcomes, such as productivity, decision making, customer service, innovative capacity, and, ultimately, profitability. The value of information and information-related activities is becoming more widely recognized, and the use of process models for evaluating information systems is gaining in prevalence (Frishammar, 2002; Choo, 2002; Davenport; 1993; McGee and Prusak; 1993).

In process management, a *process* is a sequence of value-adding stages designed to deliver a product and/or service to external and internal customers. The methodology involves conceptualizing each step and substep where value is added through a series of transformations in the process (Electronic College of Process Innovation, 2002).

The most significant process model of information management portrayed in the literature consists of six distinct steps, covering the entire information value chain of an information system. Figure 2.2 shows the information management cycle according to each of these steps: identification of information needs, information acquisition, information organization and storage development of information

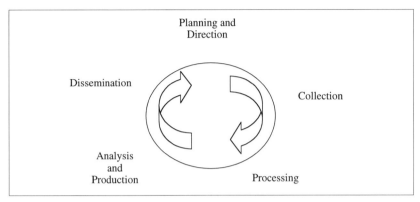

Figure 2.3   CIA Intelligence Process (CIA, 2001)

products and services (packaging), information distribution, and information use (Choo, 2002).

Each step in this model represents a distinct information-related process (step 7, adaptive behavior, is an outcome of the information process, not a step in the process). Although this model attempts to portray the entire value chain in the management of information, it must be adapted in order to correctly represent the information-related processes of intelligence systems. CI is both an information system, in that it adds value to information through a variety of activities, and an intelligence system, in that it transforms information into intelligence. The analysis of information is a prerequisite of CI and adds the most value within the CI process by attaching meaning to information, resulting in intelligence with practical import within a specific context. We discuss this process in greater detail later in the chapter.

Contrasting with the information management cycle is the intelligence cycle, conceptualized by the CIA as a continuous process with five distinct steps (see Figure 2.3).

As in the information management model discussed earlier, the CIA also conceptualizes the intelligence process as a continuous cycle, with each step feeding into the next one. However, several distinctions between this cycle and the information management cycle are apparent, the first and foremost being the inclusion of the "analysis and production" step. According to the CIA, this step involves integrating, evaluating, and analyzing all available data and preparing intelligence products. Analysts consider the information's reliability,

Table 2.2 Models of Competitive Intelligence Cycle

Information Management Cycle (Choo, 2002)	CIA (2001)	Fuld & Co. (2002)	Pirttilä (1998)	Kahaner (1998)	Miller (2000)
Identification of information needs (1)	Planning and direction (1)	Planning and direction (1)	Definition of competitors and information needs (1)	Planning and direction (1)	Identification on key decision makers and intelligence needs (1)
Information acquisition (2)	Collection (2)	Secondary/Published information sources (2)	Systematic collection of competitive information (2)	Collection (2)	Collection (2)
		Primary source collection (3)			
Organization and storage (3)	Processing (3)		Screening and analysis of collected information (3)		
	Analysis and production (4)	Analysis and production (4)		Analysis (3)	Analysis (3)
Information products and services (4)		Report and inform (5)			
Information distribution (5)	Dissemination (5)		Distribution to relevant user groups (4)	Dissemination (4)	Dissemination (4)
Information use (6)					

validity, and relevance. They integrate data into a coherent whole, put the evaluated information in context, and produce finished intelligence that includes assessments of events and judgments about the implications of the information (Central Intelligence Agency, 2001). The CIA considers the development of products, such as intelligence reports, to be part of this step.

Many conceptualizations of the CI cycle can be found in the literature. To show their similarities and differences, Table 2.2 presents the basic steps identified by several authors, each of whom divides the CI process into four to six phases.

The models presented in Table 2.2 are remarkably similar; however, some distinctive dimensions are evident. Regarding the first step, we see that, despite the different titles, each model recognizes the importance of identifying the type of intelligence/information that is needed to begin the process. Although planning should be the starting point of any process, we can argue that, in the CI cycle, planning relates mainly to the identification of the intelligence needs that must be fulfilled and of the various activities and analyses that are required to fulfill such needs.

Each model also includes a collection or acquisition stage as a second step. Only Fuld & Co. differentiates the collection of information in two parts: secondary/published and primary sources. Such a distinction is not really appropriate because, although it is important to distinguish various types of sources to develop specific gathering techniques, only one activity is involved, that of gathering information. The distinction between primary and secondary sources is also somewhat problematic and reveals the influence of market intelligence. Indeed, in marketing, primary research is conducted through focus groups or consumer surveys, and documents summarizing research results are often defined as primary sources whereas secondary sources represent published materials interpreting such research results. Primary sources are also considered by Fuld & Co. as equivalent to human sources, such as sales representatives. However, in the library and information science community, primary sources correspond to any materials containing raw and noninterpreted information that emanates from someone who is as close as possible to an event. So, first-hand documents such as diaries, court records, census data, and interviews are all considered to be primary sources. On the other hand, secondary sources are works that interpret or analyze events and are generally at least one step removed from these events. Therefore, a published source such as an article can correspond to a primary source (if it is the story of an event as reported by a journalist) as well as to a secondary source (if it is an interpretation of various stories found in primary sources). Tertiary sources, not discussed by Fuld & Co., compile information about primary or secondary sources such as directories, encyclopedias, or indexes and can be very useful in the context of CI. Associating primary sources to human sources is certainly misleading because a rumor reported by the sales representative of a competing company should be considered as a secondary source because the information has not come directly from the source. On the other hand, a published annual report can be seen as a primary source because it emanates directly from the competitor. In addition, searching for information in a Web-based environment renders the distinction between primary and secondary sources more or less irrelevant when developing acquisition strategies because both types of sources can be easily retrieved. However, it does need to be taken into account for evaluating information. In the end, we argue that the acquisition or collection of information, regardless of the specific type of information source, is a distinct step. Types of sources may differ according to information needs, but each different type does not require its own step in the CI cycle, just as different types of analytical techniques will not require their own step. That being said, collecting information from a variety of sources including employees, customers, suppliers, company Web sites, and newspapers, among others, is important in providing a more detailed picture of one's competitors and should not be simplified.

After the collection of information, the only CI cycle that identifies a step related to the processing of information is the CIA model. In comparison to the information management cycle, the organization and storage of information is a step that is regularly overlooked by the CI community. This step is key to an effective information-related system. By paying close attention to both the indexing of information and the storage architecture, users may avert the loss of stored information in a system, thus increasing access to information already collected. Although CI users rely heavily on indexing in order to find information, most know little or nothing about the skills and techniques necessary to accomplish it.

All CI models include an analysis stage. Although it is not part of the information management model, this stage is an integral part of any intelligence process. Analysis transforms information into intelligence using a variety of techniques. Pirttilä's model, which omits the organization and storage step, includes "screening" in the analysis step. The distinction between the two steps—where the organization and storage step ends and where the analysis step begins—remains vague. Analysis is a process in itself, beginning with the synthesizing and grouping together of disparate pieces of information. Only after these activities have been performed can the user transform the information into intelligence by attaching meaning, ultimately resulting in recommendation for action.

In the information management cycle, Choo (2002) posits a step for designing information products and services that does not appear in any of the CI cycle models presented here. Although this particular

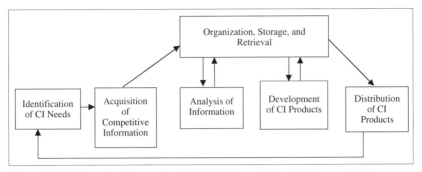

Figure 2.4   Information-Processing Model of Competitive Intelligence Cycle

task may be implicit in the CI models, it is indeed an important step. Developing products and services is often lumped together with either the analysis step or the distribution step. However, the creation of a final product for reporting intelligence is a condition for its dissemination. Different types of intelligence require different viewing formats, and the creation of these products should be distinguished from the mode by which they are distributed.

All of the CI models discussed here present the distribution or dissemination step as the last stage of the cycle. This makes sense because the value of a CI process ultimately rests on whether the final product is distributed to the appropriate decision maker at the appropriate time.

And finally, information use, which is the final step of the information management cycle, is not echoed in the CI models. It can be argued that the extent to which intelligence is used is beyond the scope of any CI unit and process.

Beyond the differences in the various models, there is a consensus that CI is a cycle because it never ends, that it is a process because it transforms something, and that it is a system when it is a formally organized management function. In addition, CI can be seen as the final outcome of the process. Therefore, it is a series of information-related activities as well as the end result of these activities.

Based on this assessment of the different models of information and intelligence systems, we have developed an information-processing model for CI (Figure 2.4). This model includes six distinctive steps, each of which represents an information-related or intelligence-related process. The idea was to incorporate relevant aspects of current information systems and intelligence systems models into one complete and comprehensive close-looped cycle for CI. This model is both more specific in its terminology (each step is labeled according to the process being applied to the information or intelligence at that stage in the model), and more comprehensive (the model includes an organization, storage, and retrieval process) than CI cycles previously described in the literature. Following, each step in the CI model is described in detail and dissected into subprocesses.

Identification of CI Needs

The terminology "identification of CI needs" was chosen to represent the major information-related activity involved in this first step. This step is crucial for ensuring a relevant CI product. Understanding the competitive intelligence needs in an organization is a complex and often difficult process that requires several key activities, as outlined in Figure 2.5.

First of all, communities of CI consumers must be identified. As discussed earlier, the nature of the information required depends, to a great deal, on who will be utilizing the outputs of CI. A highly effective CI process analyzes information to a degree that renders it unusable to those other than the target audience. Each group of clients needs CI for specific purposes, to accomplish some decision making from a certain perspective. Because the clients within one group will share similar goals, these groups are called communities. Most often, the purpose of CI is to provide intelligence for planning strategy; however, programs may also provide intelligence for other decision makers within an organization. Regardless of the location and function of the CI department, intelligence needs are continually changing, consequently, the identification and assessment of intelligence needs must be performed on a regular basis.

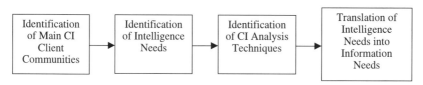

Figure 2.5   Identification of CI Needs Subprocesses

After intelligence needs have been identified, two other important aspects of this process must be completed before moving to the next step (acquiring information). Intelligence needs must be translated into the basic information requirements. To do this, it will often be necessary to first choose the analytical tool by which information will be transformed into intelligence. A practical example may help to illustrate this process. Consider a basic scenario: Senior managers want to know how their competitors will react to a price reduction on a popular product. Once the intelligence need has been identified (How will our competitors react?), it is then up to the CI department to deconstruct this into an appropriate analytical technique and to identify the information requirements for such a technique. The CI department may choose one or more analytical techniques, such as Personality Profiling, Scenario Development, or Porter's Five-Forces Model, and these analytical models will guide to a certain extent the information requirements. If the selected technique is Personality Profiling, for example, it would be necessary to collect information on specific top managers of the corporations representing the competitors, including how they behaved in the past when price reduction was announced in the industry, the corporate moves that followed, and the potential behaviors and decisions they might adopt. If the analytical technique Scenario Development is selected, then CI analysts will be required to define a number of potential scenarios (e.g., (a) some competitors also reduce their price by 10 percent; (b) all competitors reduce their price by 15 percent, etc.) and seek the information that would help to forecast the impact of these scenarios on the industry.

Table 2.3 provides more examples of the type of information needs common in the CI process, accompanied by a short description of how the information may be analyzed to produce intelligence. The list is by no means exhaustive; the needs of one company may differ from another depending on the nature of the current conditions and competitive environment.

Acquisition of Competitive Information

Once the information requirements for the CI process have been identified, the information must be collected. The acquisition of competitive information involves a number of activities and is outlined in Figure 2.6.

Table 2.3   Examples of CI Information Needs and Outcomes

CI-Related Information Needs	Potential CI Outcomes
Product announcements and pre-announcements	Features and availability indicate product strengths and gaps
Executive behavior	A person's background may provide clues about his or her decision-making style
Lawsuits and court rulings	Legal actions can indicate future liabilities
Job openings	Skills and knowledge sought may offer clues about product or strategy direction
Customer feedback	Information about perceived product strengths and (rarely) weaknesses can be derived
Suppliers or subcontractors	Partnerships or deals may show key dependencies and sources of competitive information
Prices and pricing structure	Comparison of prices and pricing structure can be used as benchmarks
Mergers, acquisitions, and strategic alliances	Signal future direction
Facilities openings and closings	Manufacturing plants are key to capacity; offices may indicate strategic direction

First, before acquiring information, it is necessary to identify potential sources of information. "The selection and use of information sources (must) be planned for, monitored, and evaluated just like any other vital resource of the organization" (Choo, 2002, p. 31). There are two important reasons for a wide variety of sources to be

Figure 2.6   Acquisition of Competitive Information Subprocesses

consulted. First, information needs of CI can be varied and complex. Second, deriving information from a variety of sources is essential for validating the accuracy of information. Information sources should be both external and internal to the organization. Internal sources include available documents, electronic files, and individuals within the organization. External sources include documents and other materials published or available from outside the organization, as well as outsiders themselves. A number of studies have shown that the majority of a company's information needs can be satisfied from within the organization (Grzanka, 1999). Despite this, many CI practitioners continue to place an emphasis on sources external to the organization to acquire information.

One valuable methodology that should be employed before beginning the acquisition process is an internal information audit, which reviews the organization's existing collection of documentation—such as records, reports, databases, and publications—and the organization's employees to determine what is already known about the competitors and their operations. This second subprocess helps to identify reliable sources within the organization, as well as to identify the gaps in knowledge about competitors. Often overlooked, employees are a rich source of competitor information, including those in sales, customer service, R&D, and particularly senior management, who often read widely, communicate with customers and suppliers, and work on a variety of projects (Choo, 2002).

Sources external to the company may be "secondary sources" such as newspaper articles or industry analysts, or "primary sources" such as financial statements or employees of competitors. Acquiring external information requires different methodologies and skills than acquiring internal information. Table 2.4 provides examples of typical sources that might be used for the identification of internal and external sources.

Once potential external and internal information sources have been identified, we reach the third subprocess of the acquisition of competitive information step. Here, two strategies can be used to acquire relevant information. First, a targeted strategy will retrieve specific pieces of information previously identified, and, second, a monitoring strategy will regularly scan the external and internal environment for pieces of information that may be relevant but were not previously identified by the targeted strategy. These two strategies suppose a number of tactics or methods for acquiring information.

Table 2.4   Typical Information Sources for CI

External Sources	Internal Sources
News databases, directories	Senior management, strategic documents
Trade journals and industry analysts reports	Marketing department, marketing plans
Trade shows, trade associations	Public relations department, press releases
Competitor Web sites	Finance and treasury, financial information
Customers, distributors, market analysts	Sales representatives, sales data
Suppliers	Human resources department, collective agreements
Competitor products and advertisements	Engineering, manufacturing, technical documents
Government agencies, legislation, regulations	Information center, internal databases

Table 2.5 presents some of these potential methods for gathering information externally and internally.

Once the information has been gathered, its content must be filtered in order to retain the desired information and discard unwanted information—the fourth subprocess of acquiring information. Filtering means examining whether the collected information addresses the needs, topics, and requirements that were identified previously. For example, if CI needs involve financial analysis of a given company, by looking at the attributes of information such as the titles, authors, or summaries of recent news stories, it is possible to filter them, retaining those that seem to be relevant and eliminating the others. The idea is to create a corpus of information by retaining what meets certain minimal requirements.

The final subprocess is assessing the validity and value of information by comparing more closely the content in order to reject inconsistent, erroneous, and redundant information. The approach here is to exclude inappropriate information. As we can see, there is only a subtle nuance between filtering and assessing, and one could argue that assessing is required before filtering. Filtering and assessing are intertwined and both involve making many decisions and value judgments. Every attempt should be made to eliminate false confirmations and misinformation, and to check for omissions and anomalies. One way of doing this is by searching for the same information in a variety of sources to examine whether it is consistent throughout the sources. The failure to test and reject what others regard as an established truth can be a major source of error. Some simple rules of thumb can be followed when evaluating the validity of information. Generally speaking, information from internal sources is harder to verify than information from published sources because it is often transferred by word of mouth and constitutes hearsay, but it also may be more valuable for the CI analysis.

Information from primary sources, or direct participants and observers (such as a statement made by a competitor's CEO), is usually more accurate than that from secondary sources such as newspapers or analyst reports, which are one step removed. However, there is no way of knowing for certain that information about a competitor is valid. As with the 2002 Enron case, even audited financial statements may prove to be incorrect or, worse, falsified. That being said, the outcome of the subprocess of acquisition of information will determine the basis for the content of the CI process.

Table 2.5   Methods for Acquiring Information

External Methods	Internal Methods
Searching information databases	Browsing documentation
Browsing trade journals and industry analysts reports	Searching internal databases
Going to trade shows	Data mining
Monitoring competitors' Web sites	Attending meetings where strategy is discussed
Surveying customers	Surveying employees
Drive-by and on-site observations	Meeting sales representatives
Interviewing external people	Interviewing key actors in the company
Reverse engineering	Soliciting news from the staff going into the field, rumors, feedback

Organization, Storage, and Retrieval

After the information has been acquired, it must be organized and stored. This part of the CI process has typically been ignored in the CI literature, presumably because information is seen as having a very short life span. The inclusion of this subprocess greatly strengthens the CI model. Once information has been determined to be useful and relevant for CI purposes, its organization and storage is crucial to facilitate its retrieval. To achieve all this, information must be indexed according to relevant topics, such as competitor, product, customer, supplier, and date of retrieval. This indexing will ensure that the information being stored is linked to other pieces of information on related subjects and can be manipulated according to the indexing structure. For example, if information is indexed according to competitor, product type, supplier, and date, the user will be able to view only information related to one competitor, or one product type, or one specific supplier, or according to the most recent information. Figure 2.7 shows the flow of information and intelligence through the organizational process.

The quality of the organization and storage process depends first and foremost on the quality of indexing applied to the material being stored. The more extensive the indexing, the higher the accuracy of information retrieval throughout the life cycle of the CI process. Indexing must be consistent and comprehensive, relying on a set of predetermined descriptors, which represent every subject of importance on which intelligence is required. The major issue in the organization of information is to create appropriate categories of topics that will be meaningful and consistent with the intelligence needs. In addition, the types of linking that will be created between records and files are determinant for information retrieval. Hierarchical linking or links showing hierarchical relationships between documents (e.g.,

Figure 2.7 Organization, Storage, and Retrieval Subprocesses

Company X → Strategic Planning → Vision Statement → Mission) and cross-topic linking (e.g., documents on various companies dealing with strategic planning should all be linked and retrievable) are necessary to ensure the successful retrieval of all relevant and related records or files.

The way the information is stored will also profoundly affect the CI process. If the information is broken down into disaggregate data and stored in identical format, greater manipulation of the data is possible and, therefore, higher level analysis may be performed. However, CI relies on qualitative information as well as quantitative information. Thus a CI system must have the ability to store information in a variety of formats, such as data, text, images, and potentially other multimedia formats.

The CI system must also be able to store information and intelligence throughout the various stages of the lifecycle of the CI process. The system should not only store acquired information but the resulting intelligence and intelligence products.

It is difficult to draw the line between where the "organization and storage" function ends and "analysis" begins in the CI process. The most basic activities of any analysis are synthesizing, filtering, and organizing, which are partly performed in this step.

This third step of the CI process is one in which software can play a significant role (Choo, 2002). As with any information system, the inability to find stored information can have severe consequences to an organization. Both quality indexing procedures and sophisticated search tools can help to avert the loss of stored information in any system.

Analysis of Information

Called, by some, the brain of the CI system, analysis is the key process that transforms information into intelligence (Herring, 1998; Werther, 2001). Figure 2.8 shows how information must be first organized and synthesized, then with inference to action, it will result in intelligence. As discussed in the previous chapter, for information to become intelligence, an inference about the meaning of the information must be made. In the literature, there is some dispute as to the level of inference required. Herring (1998) defines "intelligent analysis" as a step in the production of intelligence in

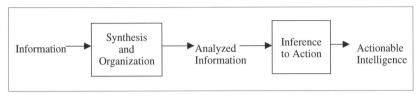

Figure 2.8 The Analysis Process

which information is subjected to systematic examination in order to identify relevant facts, determine significant relationships, and derive key findings and conclusions.

Westney and Ghoshal (1994) describe the basic process of analysis as synthesis, hypothesis, and the specification and testing of the assumptions underlying them. Both of these descriptions take a more conservative approach to the level of inference required. The main outcome of CI is a set of hypothetical results (in terms of gains, sales, advantages, and disadvantages) based on a number of possible strategic actions that could be taken by an enterprise. For example, "if we lower the price of our product, how will our competitors react, and what impact might their reaction have on our organization?" In fact, analysis involves asking questions and developing hypotheses about the answer for each question (O'Guin and Ogilvie, 2001). For others, the inference should go beyond hypothesis to recommendations to action (Fuld & Co., 2000). For example, "based on the competitor profiles we have established, we should lower the price of our product." This level of inference requires an expert system with a built-in knowledge base (probably in finance, psychology, management, etc.) in which the inputs are the competitive conditions, and an inference mechanism uses the built-in knowledge base to make a decision about what kind of action should be taken. Expert systems are extremely costly to produce because they require a large knowledge base to be developed, and, to date, there exists no software system that performs this level of inference in the CI function (Fuld & Co., 2002).

The analysis process is considered to be the most important step in the CI cycle, but it is also the process most difficult to describe. Many formal analytical techniques are employed by CI practitioners—one practitioner counted over 100 (Herring, 1998)—and sophisticated techniques such as data mining and statistical methods such as cluster analysis can be used to extract more meaning from data

(Marín-Llanes et al., 2001). But analysis is also often done in an informal way in the minds of analysts. A 1998 study surveyed CI practitioners about the most effective analysis techniques for CI. Respondents revealed that the eight most effective techniques were SWOT analysis, competitor profiles, cost/financial analysis, win/loss analysis, war gaming, scenario development, conjoint analysis, and simulation/modeling (Powell and Allgaier, 1998). Following are descriptions of several of these methods as described in the CI and strategic planning literature:

- Benchmarking. This technique involves comparing the attributes of your competitor with those of your own company to help identify where you can improve. The gaps that result, known as positive or negative gaps, identify areas where your company may be performing better than or worse than your competitor (Sandman, 2000).

- SWOT. This technique places a company's internal strengths and weaknesses in a matrix format, along with external opportunities and threats. The technique offers a big-picture view of a competitor and the competitive environment in which it is operating. It is useful in determining a competitor's weak spots and, conversely, determining strategic opportunities (Fuld, 1995; Lang, 2001; Sandman, 2000).

- Personality Profiling. This analytical method is based on the theory that the actions of a company will, to a certain extent, depend on the personality of its top executives. Personality profiling studies three key aspects of a competitor's CEO (Kahaner, 1998): (1) the past successes and failures of the CEO—based on the theory that previous actions predict future actions, (2) the behavioral traits of the CEO—based on the theory that people who take personal risks will also take business risks, and (3) the current business environment— based on the theory that a CEO is likely to react differently depending on the corporate culture within which he or she is working. From this information, one can better predict the future actions of a competitor.

- Competitor Profiling. This method of analysis is the most common type of analysis used in CI (Fuld, 1995; Sandman, 2000; Wells, 2001). However, this broad term actually refers to a number of more specific types of profiling, such as the personality profiling described above. Other attributes of a competitor that are profiled are financial statements, manufacturing processes, staff and facilities, and products. In fact, any aspect of a competitor may be profiled using "competitor profiling" to gain a better understanding of the characteristics of that competitor, depending on the context of the analysis.

- Patent Analysis. At its most basic, this technique involves discovering competitors' patents in order to determine the new technologies being developed. Reviewing such patents can provide links to previous patents and shed light on a firm's long-term strategies (Castells et al., 2000).

- War Gaming. Based on an old military technique, this type of analysis assigns players in the "game" to act as competitors or as themselves, and asks them to explore various strategies through role play. The goal is to gain insight into potential responses to strategic moves by one's competitors (Kurtz, 2000).

Of the literally hundreds of potential analytical techniques available, this listing describes some of the more popular ones. (For more information, see *CI Analytical Tools: How Effective Are They?* on the SCIP Web site.) New techniques are also being developed such as Channels-to-Market Mapping, which uses marketing concepts to address tactical and strategic decisions (Bulger, 2001). Each technique will provide the company with a different snapshot of its competitive environment, and each technique will have its own set of information requirements. It is therefore critically important that the analytical techniques being used are determined at the beginning of the CI process and are linked to the identification of information needs process. Because no single CI analytical technique can provide a full picture of the competitive environment, a thorough CI process will employ several. The techniques chosen will depend on the nature of the competitive environment. A personality profile may be conducted when a competitor hires a new CEO, for example, or a cost analysis may be performed when a competitor is able to sell products at a lower price.

The amount of value added in the analysis stage is greater than that in any other step of the CI cycle. Because information in this step is manipulated, examined, condensed, or expanded—to a large extent to add meaning and inference—it is transformed into intelligence. It has, after this process, a significantly higher use value for the company.

Development of Intelligence Products

The packaging of CI as a product for distribution is a very important step in the CI cycle. Depending on the audience and the nature of the intelligence, one report format may be more effective than another. Senior management often does not have time to read lengthy reports and some types of analysis, such as benchmarking, are better delivered in graph, chart, or table format. The intelligence to be presented may be a single piece of information to add to the big picture—for instance, a news story that changes the response profile of a competitor, or an in-depth personality profile of a competitor's CEO. An effective CI system should provide a flexibility and range of product formats. Although some may view the development of intelligence products as a simple word processing function because it involves designing reports, it will require a number of decisions on the part of CI professionals. To deliver good products, CI professionals must decide which format will best convey the analysis done, reveal the critical assessment of information, and will indicate the limitations of information sources. The delivery of well-packaged CI products requires a thorough analysis of intelligence needs and the particular information-seeking behavior of CI clients.

Distribution of Intelligence Products

Distributing intelligence to those who need it is the final process in the CI cycle. Even the most insightful intelligence is useless if it fails to reach the right people to take action. This step often requires the dissemination of information to various individuals within the organization, at various stages of the process, and with varying degrees of detail—getting the right information to the right person at the right time (Choo, 2002). The key issue is to assure that all those who could benefit from the intelligence are given efficient and timely access. A number of channels may be used to distribute CI, including face-to-face conversation, telephone, e-mail, and posting on the company intranet. As in the information packaging process, the value of the distribution method is directly related to the consumer and to the nature of the intelligence being communicated. A good CI system will allow for a variety of distribution channels and the flexibility to select the appropriate one.

This completes the description of the various steps involved in this information processing CI model. By deconstructing CI into its various information-related processes and subprocesses, it is possible to reach a better understanding of the CI function. The CI model presented here is based on a number of important assumptions about the nature of competitive intelligence, as discussed earlier in this chapter. First of all, CI is a continuous and iterative cycle of six steps, each of which adds value to the CI product as it moves through these steps. These six steps include (1) identifying the CI needs in the organization, (2) acquiring the needed information, (3) organizing and storing the information, (4) transforming the information into intelligence through analysis, (5) creating competitive intelligence products, and (6) distributing those products to the CI consumer. Second, the CI consumer has historically been the strategic planning department, which requires a high level of analysis in order to predict the future movements of competitors based on a variety of strategic directions. Third, CI includes the analysis of all aspects of a competitor that may affect the ability of the organization to compete. Finally, depending on the competitive environment of a particular industry, the scope of CI needs to be examined carefully.

Identifying the Value-Added Processes of Competitive Intelligence Software

Information technology is playing an unprecedented role in our lives today. We have become reliant on many devices for the handling of information and the staggering rate of technological change continues to augment the role of technology in our lives. It is amazing that technology such as the World Wide Web, created in 1991, is now used by millions of people and is as common as the telephone in the Western World. The information technology marketplace offers a large variety of software applications for storing, retrieving, filtering, summarizing, translating, e-mailing, or customizing information, as is described in Chapter 4. Existing software applications are being replaced continuously by new versions, and new technology is developed on a regular basis. Why should we bother assessing new technological products if they will soon be replaced by updated and improved versions and if new technologies are always on the horizon?

In fact, it is the landscape of technological diversity that justifies the need for a more critical assessment of products. Although these innovations attempt to better address the requirements of various types of users, the question remains to what extent technological improvements contribute to better meet these requirements. In the area of CI alone, one organization has identified close to 289 associated software applications (CI Resource, http://CISeek.com). The question arises: How can we assess such a large quantity of potentially useful technologies, and on what basis? Similarly, how can the average user make sense of such diverse applications? These questions become even more important if user requirements are not clear, well defined, and agreed upon by software engineers or even by experts. Given the fact that CI represents a recent phenomenon in many countries and is almost a tradition in others, the way it is practiced varies greatly. CI professionals and managers may have very different expectations and interpretations of the outcomes of the CI process and of the technological support that should be available to them.

Many possible approaches are available to evaluate information technology in general, and information retrieval systems in particular; that is, systems that are used to store and retrieve information. One of the basic dimensions of any software evaluation is whether the purpose of the technology has been addressed sufficiently in its development, or, in other words, whether a user can achieve the intended goals when using a given product. In CI technology, the first step should be to examine whether the application helps to support the CI cycle. As we have seen, the CI cycle and its scope are not definitive and are viewed differently by different people.

The evaluation criteria presented in this chapter are based on our conceptual framework of CI and evolved out of our information-processing approach to CI. These criteria are aimed at identifying the value-added processes that should take place when using a CI software application to transform information into intelligence. The next section provides a brief overview of approaches used to evaluate software. Of note is the obvious lack of studies evaluating software based on the value-added processes. We then present our set of criteria based on Taylor's (1986) approach.

Evaluating Information Technology

Information technology includes both the hardware and software used to handle information. The evaluation of such technology has been a concern in many areas of research, including management of information systems, human–computer interaction, information management, and information retrieval. Information systems are usually aimed at supporting various organizational operations as well as decision making. Information retrieval (IR) systems, a subset of information systems, are mainly designed to store and retrieve information. IR systems were among the first applications of computers more than 40 years ago. Today they can handle not only bibliographic and numerical data, but also full-text and multimedia documents. Evaluation of IR systems has been a major area of research in computer and information science. However, it remains a challenge for investigators because, as acknowledged by Tague-Sutcliffe (1996), Hersh (1998), and Morse (2002), a lack of consensus persists about both the methodologies to be employed as well as the exact nature of IR systems (Dunlop, 2000). The purpose of evaluating IR systems was and remains to be the improvement of the information retrieval process and increased user satisfaction (Tague-Sutcliffe, 1996). Research in this area has generated a large body of literature promoting either system-oriented methodologies (with a focus on the technical features and the performance of the systems) or user-centered methodologies (with an emphasis on how users interact with the systems and how they perceive their outputs). It is widely agreed that there is a need to use a variety of innovative methodologies when evaluating information retrieval systems. Illustrating this are some major research initiatives, such as the Defense Advanced Research Projects Agency's (DARPA) Information Management Program, which supports the exploration of alternative evaluation methods (Morse, 2002), and the Text Retrieval Conferences (TREC), sponsored by the National Institute of Standards and Technology and DARPA, which, since 1994, have been providing a setting for large-scale testing of text retrieval technology (Voorhees and Harman, 2001).

System-oriented methodologies have dominated the scene, especially the study of information system efficiencies in terms of recall and precision (Dunlop, 2002; Harter and Hert, 1998). These studies focus on the measurement of relevance, or the "subject relatedness" and "the utility" of a record for a given user (Meadow et al., 2000). The idea is to assess what can be retrieved from a system or database (recall), and to what extent these results are relevant from a subject perspective and/or a user perspective (precision). "Recall" is the ratio that indicates the number of relevant records retrieved to the total number of relevant records existing in the database or the capacity to retrieve relevant documents, while "precision" is the ratio of relevant records retrieved in relation to the total number of records retrieved, or the capacity to avoid the retrieval of nonrelevant documents. At the heart of these measurements lies the notion of relevance and how relevance judgments should be established, either with real users or with computational techniques that anticipate users' judgments. Traditionally, the evaluation of IR systems is based on a simplistic view of relevance (document is relevant or not), which assumes that relevance is mainly topical (when the topic of the document matches the topic of the query). This approach to evaluation involves mainly experiments in artificial environments without real users, and raised a number of criticisms as explained by Large et al. (1999).

User-oriented studies are concerned with factors other than topical relevance and examine the performance of systems in relation to users' characteristics, knowledge, needs, and information seeking behavior (Ellis et al., 2002). Evaluation based on a user-centered approach does not focus on system effectiveness only but also on how users actually search information and on their satisfaction regarding the outcomes of the search. The development of this type of evaluation over the past two decades recognizes that IR systems are more interactive; when searching information, users interact with a human or/and computer intermediary and systems send various signals to users who can then modify their strategies (Ellis et al., 2002). To illustrate the values inherent in the system-oriented and the user-oriented approaches to evaluation, Dunlop (2000) uses an interesting car analogy. While evaluating the performance of the engine in terms of power output and fuel efficiency is essential, it is also important to consider factors addressing their suitability for the drivers, such as comfort and storage capacity.

CI software should hardly be evaluated in terms of the recall and precision of outcomes alone. On one hand, recall and precision implies the concept of relevance and, given the changing nature of competitive conditions and CI needs, the relevance of competitive information might vary accordingly. In addition, as Mizzaro (1998) suggests, various categories of relevance (topic, task, and context) would lead to differing assessments of the value of a piece of information. Chen et al. (2002) argue that methods relying on recall and precision do not capture how users understand the content of retrieved documents and how relevance is actually assessed. In the context of CI, factors such as time or money might be equally as important to the user as topical relevance. The outcomes of a CI system are very difficult to assess because competitive information changes constantly. Unlike a database having a fairly constant number of records that are organized and can be later retrieved, CI systems must be constantly updated, integrating new records and data regularly. The information stored in CI systems must be reviewed on a current basis, in light of new intelligence needs. As well, CI systems are more than information retrieval systems. They should also assist users in conducting various types of analysis. Such systems, which will yield very different outcomes in terms of formats (reports) and content (conclusions), must take into account specific situations, contexts, and needs, and require assessment techniques beyond those offered in the IR evaluation methodologies we have described here.

With the increased popularity of desktop software applications, and with the growing sophistication of both hardware and software, the need for evaluation criteria other than those linked to system effectiveness, such as recall and precision, has been addressed. Sieverts and Hofstede (1994) propose eight categories of evaluation criteria: technical requirements, special versions and security, use of the program, limitations, input and maintenance of data, indexing of stored information, retrieval of stored information, and output of data. Within each of these categories are more specific criteria, which help to examine how the system functions from a technical point of view and whether the outputs are satisfying from a user perspective. Richards (1995) organizes evaluation criteria into four categories, also with text retrieval in mind. The top-level criteria include functions related to searching the database and accounts for 80 percent of the evaluation. Operational criteria refer to the execution of tasks and movement between menus. Navigation criteria include moving between and within records. Ergonomics criteria deal with the layout of screens, use of color, and terminology used. To evaluate software from a system-oriented approach there is an obvious need to use criteria that are related to the mechanisms of the software, or its technical features, and to the global task or function for which the software was designed—for instance, matching documents to queries in the case of text retrieval systems. The general evaluation criteria suggested by these authors are not helpful in evaluating CI software because they do not address the particular purpose of information retrieval in the context of CI.

Taking a more user-oriented approach, the field of human–computer interaction (HCI) has generated much interest in assessing the usability and acceptability of software applications, which has contributed to a vast body of literature. The term "usability" refers to the quality or ease of use of a given product (Bevan, 1995). When the concept was first introduced, usability was mainly product oriented and measured in terms of the ergonomic attributes of a product. Today, usability involves also the measurement of the mental effort required by the user (user-oriented view) and the interaction between the user and the product in terms of usefulness and ease of use (user-performance view). Usability is a major design objective for all products, including information retrieval systems (Shneiderman, 1998) and Web technology (Nielsen, 2000; Nielsen and Tahir, 2001). A badly designed interface can contribute to human error and user dissatisfaction (Zhang and von Dran, 2000). A series of ISO standards (as promoted by the International Organization for Standardization) have been developed to deal with software quality and usability, and today the number one recommendation is to opt for user-centered design. Therefore, various methods are recommended for measuring product usability at the design stage as well as once the product has been completed (observation of users, interviews, questionnaires, simulations, think aloud protocol, etc.). This type of evaluation is useful, for instance, to improve the interface, the capacity of the software to be customized (both in terms of functions and interface), and to better document the help function.

Again, although these criteria are useful for evaluating information retrieval software, they are not helpful for assessing commercial products for CI because the context of CI is not taken into account. The context represents that portion of the system for which the product should exhibit fitness (Carney and Wallnau, 1998). Metzger et al. (1998) also consider that, ideally, software design should be conducted on the basis of user needs, while taking into account the nature of the particular tasks and activities that users must undertake. However, few evaluation studies have tried to address the fitness of IR system in performing the particular tasks desired by users. Fuld & Co. (1998; 2000; 2002) did some pioneering work regarding the evaluation of CI software by analyzing and scoring such products for a number of years. Claiming to use over 120 criteria, Fuld & Co. (2002) examines technical fitness related to each step of the CI cycle (as presented in Table 2.2). For example, regarding the "Planning and Direction" step, one criterion contends to assess whether the software has the capability of receiving requests from employees within the company. For the step "Published Information Collection," a criterion addresses whether the software can search in various information repositories. Fuld & Co. employs evaluation criteria that measure a system's CI fitness or its ability to perform the CI function, as a proper evaluation of CI software should; however, the firm does not explain all the criteria used in its evaluation: Twenty-seven of 120 are described in its 2002 report. In addition, Fuld & Co. and most other investigators conducting evaluation studies of CI systems do not specifically examine the value-added processes aimed at transforming information into intelligence that should characterize CI software. Examining the various technical features of CI software is important—however, if these features are not assessed in the light of the value they add to information, they will not help a user to determine whether a software application is useful for the CI function.

A unique set of criteria for the product's fitness based on its purpose and on the particular needs of the consumer would constitute the ideal scenario, but the development of customized evaluation measures is time-consuming and often beyond the ability of end-users. Hence, the development of a standard set of criteria to establish the basic fitness of a given software product to perform CI is needed in order to aid the end-user.

Before considering appropriate criteria, the first question that must be answered is: What are the tasks involved in CI? Given that the major objective of CI is to add value to information for specific purposes, the tasks involved in CI are to define these purposes, to collect information accordingly, to store and organize it for later efficient retrieval, to process and analyze it, to prepare various documents by manipulating the results, and to distribute these documents to decision makers. All of these tasks can be combined to define the function of a CI software application.

The next question is: Who should perform each of these tasks? For instance, CI analysts, managers at various organizational levels, and entrepreneurs may all be interested in using a CI software application. Thus, the application should be adaptable to the needs and characteristics of a variety of user groups within an organization, including those with little or no CI experience.

After a review of the CI and software evaluation literature, and with these questions in mind, we have compiled a short list of criteria used to evaluate general software applications: ability to fulfill purpose, interface design, compatibility with hardware and other software, technical expertise required, and usefulness of help facility. A comprehensive set of CI-specific criteria was also developed to address one important criterion, the ability of software to fulfill its stated purpose. This criterion was expanded based on our CI model defined in Chapter 2 and value-added processes as defined by Taylor (1986).

As we have seen in Chapter 1, Taylor's model is interesting for two main reasons. First, it involves a user-centered perspective taking into account simple and basic user criteria for assessing information systems. Second, a real attempt is made in this model to identify the value-added processes that should be inherent in any information system, recognizing that adding value to information should be the main goal of such a system. Considering that the goal of CI is the production of value-added information, Taylor's framework is highly applicable. Our goal here is to show how it is relevant to CI software.

Based on a previous comparative analysis of CI software conducted in 2000, we developed a set of 35 evaluation criteria (Bouthillier and Shearer, 2001a, 2001b). These criteria were reviewed and refined in 2002 in the light of new technological developments. The revised set of 32 criteria will be presented in the next section. The criteria are grouped according to the information process to which they are related and have been assigned user-oriented criteria.

Targeting the Value-Added Dimensions

Few authors have tried to determine the value-added dimensions involved in CI. Westney and Ghoshal (1994) made an interesting contribution using an information processing approach. After interviewing 73 analysts, 17 managers of analysts, 63 CI clients, and eight information technology specialists, they developed a three-dimensional model of the information value-adding chain of CI. The first dimension is *data management*, consisting of 10 processes: acquisition, classification, storage, retrieval, editing, verification and quality control, presentation of data, aggregation, distribution, and assessment based on clients' reactions to the output of CI. The second dimension is *analysis* (synthesis, development of hypothesis, and assumption building and creating), and the third is labeled *implication*—expressing the fact that management must, at the end of the CI process, assess how to respond to the outcomes of the analysis. This model was not aimed at assessing the potential of CI software; it was supported, nevertheless, by their study, which provides useful data revealing basic CI corporate practices that will be presented here.

As previously mentioned, Fuld & Co. (1998, 2000, 2002) regularly evaluates intelligence software based on a CI model described in Chapter 2. The 27 criteria made public in the firm's most recent report (Fuld & Co., 2002) are not expressed in terms of value-added dimensions but instead target the technical features of the products. For example, the criteria related to the "Planning and Direction" step examine whether a system provides a framework to input Key Intelligence Topics and Questions (KITs and KIQs) or whether it allows for collaborative work. The criteria for the "Published Information Collection" step assess the internal and external search capabilities, the automatic filtering of collected information, and so on. Most of these criteria are perfectly relevant—however, the fact that there are 93 other criteria left unidentified leaves potential buyers of these products in a difficult position, relying on the opinions of Fuld & Co. rather than on their ability to assess the products for themselves. Thus, the development of a manageable list of criteria should be of interest to many. This will give end-users the option of conducting their own evaluation of CI software products and allow them to make a final assessment about the appropriateness of an application.

Taylor's model of value-added processes represents a powerful framework for examining the capabilities of information systems. These value-added processes are also applicable to CI software because such software should add value through converting information into intelligence. Moreover, Taylor's model allows the integration of a system-oriented approach with both task-oriented and user-centered perspectives. Table 3.1 presents a list of 38 criteria; 32 of these criteria are related to CI and are broken down into the six types of processes characterizing CI accompanied by their corresponding user-oriented criteria and the values involved as defined by Taylor. An explanation of the meanings and relationships between these criteria follow.

Identification of CI Needs

The first category of value-added processes deals with the potential of a system to meet the specific information needs of different CI users. Considering that the application should help to develop an appropriate CI system, it should contribute to defining and refining these needs. This step resembles what is accomplished by a librarian when conducting a reference interview. The librarian, without necessarily being an expert in the field, helps to translate the information problems of a client into information needs and requirements by taking into account the client's context, background, constraints, and preferences. This is achieved by asking a number of questions to the client to refine the topic(s) and the type of information needed as well as the amount of information required. But, before this can be accomplished, the main consumer of the CI must be identified. *Identification of main CI client communities* consists of locating the major groups in the organization that require CI. An application should then help to identify them by

Table 3.1 Evaluation Criteria for CI Software

Evaluation Criteria Value-Added Processes	User Criteria (Taylor)	Values Involved (Taylor)
I. Identification of CI needs		
1. Identification of main CI client communities	Adaptability	Closeness to problem
2. Identification of CI topics	Ease of use/noise reduction	Interfacing/selectivity
3. Translation of CI topics into specific information requirements	Noise reduction	Precision/selectivity
4. Identification of CI analytical techniques	Ease of use/noise reduction	Interfacing/selectivity
5. Capability to change CI topics and techniques	Adaptability	Flexibility
II. Acquisition of competitive information		
6. Identification of external information sources	Noise reduction	Linkage/selectivity
7. Identification of internal information sources	Noise reduction	Linkage/selectivity
8. Identification of sources for specific topics	Noise reduction	Linkage/selectivity
9. Monitoring content within information sources	Quality	Currency
10. Monitoring information sources	Quality	Currency
11. Targeting of information within sources	Noise reduction	Precision
12. Filtering information content	Noise reduction	Access
13. Alerting of information	Quality/adaptability	Currency/stimulatory
14. Importation of information	Ease of use	Physical accessibility
15. Screening of information	Noise reduction	Selectivity
16. Rating of information	Noise reduction	Selectivity
III. Organization, storage, and retrieval		
17. Indexing	Noise reduction	Intellectual access
18. Hierarchical linking	Ease of use	Ordering
19. Cross-topic linking	Ease of use	Ordering
20. Storage of variety of formats	Ease of use/adaptability	Formatting/flexibility
21. Storage capacity	Ease of use	Physical accessibility
22. Internal searching	Noise reduction	Precision
23. Browsing	Ease of use	Browsing
IV. Analysis of information		
24. Variety of CI analytical techniques	Adaptability	Closeness to the problem
25. Level of analysis	Quality	Comprehensiveness
26. Synthesis of information	Noise reduction	Intellectual access
27. Recommendations for action	Quality	Validity
V. Development of CI products		
28. Variety of formats for viewing CI products	Ease of use	Formatting

29. Effectiveness of formats	Adaptability/quality	Simplicity/validity
30. Flexibility for adapting CI products	Adaptability	Flexibility
VI. Distribution of CI products		
31. Capacity for distributing CI products	Ease of use	Physical accessibility
32. Identification of potential CI consumers	Adaptability	Closeness to problem

Other general criteria		
1. Ease of use of the interface	Ease of use	Interfacing
2. Capability for changing display	Adaptability	Flexibility
3. Navigation features	Ease of use	Browsing
4. Software compatibility	Adaptability	Flexibility
5. Usefulness of help facility	Ease of use	Interfacing
6. Requirement of technical expertise	Ease of use	Interfacing

suggesting potential sets of users: the corporate planning unit, the marketing department, the economic analysis department, or the research and development group, for example. If an application has that capability, it would meet the user criterion *adaptability*, or the set of mechanisms to strengthen the responsiveness of the system to specific user problems, and it would add the value *closeness to problem* by addressing specific user needs in a particular environment.

The next criterion is *Identification of CI topics*. Once the CI clients have been identified, the system should help to identify the specific topics about which information must be collected. Presumably, people working in strategic planning will require different types of intelligence on competitors than say, in research and development (e.g., corporate strategies versus pending patents). This function is fundamental to the setup of a good CI system. *Translation of CI topics into specific information requirements*, the next step, seeks to translate broader intelligence topics into basic information requirements. For example, the topic "corporate strategies" implies seeking information on moves, mergers, acquisitions, or partnerships, whereas "marketing strategies" will require information on pricing, packaging, publicity, or distribution.

Translating CI topics into information requirements involves making recommendations about the various pieces of information needed. These terms also represent potential search terms to use when making queries. The application should help to define the terminology (synonyms and related terms), a form of controlled vocabulary that can be utilized when searching information. This feature is particularly important if the CI system is managed by an inexperienced searcher.

Identification of CI analytical techniques involves defining from the outset the types of analysis required. This activity connects the information needs with the CI topics. For example, the CI topic of financial analysis can be performed using a variety of analytical techniques, such as profitability ratios or benchmarking. Different analytical techniques also require the collection of different types of information. Thus, not only does the CI topic affect the information requirements, but so does the analytical technique chosen.

The three latter criteria are related to *noise reduction*. This is a very important dimension from a user perspective because it is connected to the idea of reducing the information universe (overload) and implies three processes: excluding information, inclusion or supplying information within predefined boundaries, and precision or focusing on specific data or information. *Selectivity* is the value added by all these steps, according to Taylor's terminology, meaning that the choices being made at the input side of the system provide some guarantee that the selected information will be appropriate and relevant. The translation of CI topics into information requirements also addresses *precision* because this factor would allow more focus for ulterior information-related activities. The two criteria, *Identification of CI topics* and *Identification of CI analytical techniques,* increase the *ease of use* by making the CI system easier to organize and augment the value *interfacing.* The *Capability to change CI topics and techniques* raises the need for *adaptability* and its value *flexibility*, enabling the user of the CI application to work dynamically with the information and the CI user requirements. Flexibility is crucial given the iterative dimension of CI. The evaluation criteria in this category help to assess whether CI technology is useful for identifying the who (clients), the what (information requirements), the why (topics), and the how (analytical techniques).

Acquisition of Competitive Information

According to the study undertaken by Westney and Ghoshal (1994), acquiring information is considered by CI analysts to be the most tedious part of their job. In that respect, software applications that can collect information automatically are in great demand, and this explains why we offer 10 evaluation criteria in this area (the largest subset of criteria of any step in the CI process). The study also revealed that CI analysts used internal sources more often than external ones, and the most commonly cited external source was external publications and documents.

Fuld & Co. (2002) suggests that information must be collected in published sources and among primary sources, or contacts with individuals within or outside an organization. We prefer to divide the types of sources into external sources (newspapers, magazines, commercial databases, grey literature, government sources, and individuals from outside the organization) and internal sources (corporate documents, organizational data, and employees). This division suggests that organizational boundaries are more critical in determining a certain type of access—in terms of collection methods, speed, ease of use, and currency—to information, than the published or human nature of the source. Collecting internal information, such as an internal report or an opinion of a sales representative, implies a very different strategy for acquiring information than that used for gathering information outside the organization (at trade shows, from consultants, or even on the Web).

At this stage, it is also important to appreciate the richness and nature of the information environment of the sector in which the organization evolves. Some sectors are known as information-rich external environments, meaning that events pertaining to that industry are well covered in the media. For example, the information technology industry or the automobile industry receives more media attention than the photographic materials industry, which is an information-lean environment (Westney and Ghoshal, 1994). The strategy needed for information acquisition will be affected by the nature of an information environment because of the varying availability of information sources. The need to study the "information use environment," or the information environment of particular groups of users, has also been recognized by Taylor (1991). Groups of users operate in information environments that have specific characteristics that should be understood before deploying information acquisition strategies.

One obvious purpose of a CI application should be to help identify typical external and internal information sources. *Identification of external information sources* and *Identification of internal information sources* are the first two criteria in this category. *Identification of sources for specific topics* should help to retrieve more specialized sources for narrow topics. These three criteria address *noise reduction*, as explained previously. Taylor's values added by these processes are *linkage*, because they provide pointers and expand the options for information acquisition, and *selectivity*, given their potential to ensure the appropriateness of the selected information. For inexperienced searchers, these three processes are essential, and they should help to refine the searching strategies of experienced CI specialists as well.

The collection of information can be achieved with several other processes. *Monitoring of content within information sources* refers to the capability of an application to recognize changes in the content of an information source in order to retrieve any new content. Every day the content of Web sites, news sources, and business information sources changes and it is necessary for CI systems to incorporate the new content in a timely fashion into their CI products. On the other hand, *Monitoring information sources* is the task of locating new sources of competitor information, such as new electronic sources (new databases, grey reports) and Web sites that might provide information on competitors and other CI topics. This task also involves monitoring the disappearance of sources. The goal of both activities is to remain as informed as possible about the information requirements for CI. Both of these tasks ensure the *quality* of the CI system by constantly seeking new information and sources, thus adding the value of *currency*. *Targeting of information within sources* implies searching, on a regular basis or on particular occasions, in information sources such as commercial business information databases (e.g., Dialog, LexisNexis, Factiva, Onesource, etc.) and internal databases (e.g., on government or other organization Web sites) by repeating similar queries. *Filtering of information*, according to Taylor (1986), is the process of compressing large amounts of information by providing, for example, the table of contents of a book, the abstract of an article, or some description of the information source's contents such as the first paragraph of a piece of information with search terms highlighted. Information seekers typically use these types of cues when deciding whether to acquire a piece of information, rather than looking at the entire content. Filtering, as explained in Chapter 2, is closely related to the assessment of information, which is aimed at rejecting redundant, repetitive, and incorrect information as well as evaluating its validity and value. However, before assessing, it is essential to highlight what might be of value in a given source. When dealing with electronic sources, filtering often means considering some parts of a document (the title and the author of an article or the table of contents of a report) to provide just enough information about the information retrieved to facilitate its consumption and its assessment. Again, targeting and filtering address the user criterion of *noise reduction*. The former adds the value *precision* by trying to find precisely what the CI user wants, and the latter contributes the value *access* because it facilitates access to information.

Alerting of information refers to the capability of alerting users to new information content. Push technology, for example, enables the system to make the user aware of any new real-time information as it is released, on the basis of predetermined topics, ensuring that the most up-to-date information will be gathered by the system. This process meets two user criteria, *quality* and *adaptability*, and adds two values, *currency* and *stimulatory*, because it alerts clients to new developments. Another criterion in this step is *Importation of information*. This refers to the mechanics of adding information to the system. What capability does the system offer for importing different formats, such as articles, advertisements, e-mail messages, Web pages, charts, graphs, pictures, or patents? From a user point of view this importation ability facilitates *ease of use* and ensures *physical accessibility*.

Screening of information assesses mainly the redundancy or repetitiveness of information. Without this process, information alerts or importation of information can be the source of information overload or, worse, can cause the retrieval of large amounts of redundant information. These two minimal forms of information assessment guarantee the value of *selectivity* by keeping only useful information and by not accepting in the system the same information twice. Ideally the assessment of information should involve the examination of the source authority and an appreciation of its universal quality, but this can hardly be achieved automatically.

Rating of information is also an important feature in information acquisition. Information that is acquired does not always have the same usefulness and relevance; similarly, the validity varies. A number of potential aspects on which one may want to rate the acquired information include the according of a simple scale of usefulness (e.g., very useful, less useful, potentially useful) to facilitate its organization, storage, and retrieval. Likewise, CI practitioners may find it helpful to rate information according to how sure they are as to its validity (e.g., rumor, opinion, fact). Such ratings can hardly be accomplished automatically because they require judgment, but would save time for the manager of the CI system when a particular piece of information is needed. Instead of reading all documents, for example, checking the rating would lead more easily to relevant documents. Although systems are not capable of rating per se, they can offer a facility for users to rate incoming information based on their judgments.

Organization, Storage, and Retrieval

For CI, as with all other information-related activities, access to information is critical. Collecting information is useless unless it is properly organized. The major advantages to implementing a CI software application is that it will integrate all the processes related to information handling. The need for a central CI storage repository in organizations has been raised often. Methods of classification and indexing are generally not well understood by CI analysts and CI clients (Westney and Ghoshal, 1994). Standardizing these methods is certainly a key issue. The organization, storage, and retrieval of information are three interrelated yet distinct processes. To begin with, organization of information implies three value-added processes: indexing, hierarchical linking, and cross-topic linking.

Indexing consists of attaching one or more descriptors, or tags, to a document or a file for later retrieval. Such a task facilitates the *intellectual access* to information. However, indexing alone is not sufficient to create a comprehensive CI system. There is a need to establish other logical relations between documents.

Hierarchical linking refers to the establishment of links among various files that are related in a hierarchical way. A hierarchy must be established, for example, between various documents such as a press release dealing with the president of an airplane manufacturer, a newspaper article about the same company, and a report describing the civil aviation and aerospace industries in which the company operates. Without hierarchical linking, retrieval of the press release by using the president's name as a search term would not lead to the identification of the two other documents, causing an inadequate exploitation of the information database. Links involving a hierarchy are also required when documents are filed in subdirectories that are themselves saved in directories.

Cross-topic linking is needed to retrieve documents that are multi-topic. Documents filed under company names might deal with other topics such as profitability ratios or environmental regulations. To study a given industry it might be essential to retrieve all the documents in which profitability ratios are discussed, regardless of the company names. Both types of linking address the need for *ease of use* and the value *ordering*, by grouping documents and by creating a certain order.

Two major issues are involved in the storage of information. An application should allow the storage of diverse formats (e.g., Word, Excel, PDF, HTML, and multimedia documents) and the storage of both collected information and the results of the analysis (the intelligence reports and other CI products such as tables, graphs, etc.). *Storage of variety of formats* is essential because CI works with numerical data, textual information, pictures, and other formats, and produces a variety of outputs, such as graphs, reports, and charts, as well. This process adds two values: *formatting,* or the possibility of storing and arranging documents in ways that would facilitate their scanning, and *flexibility,* for the potential for a dynamic manipulation of files. *Storage capacity* will determine the value *physical accessibility,* and it would be added when the software application should enable the system manager to create a database incorporating collected information and intelligence products for easier access and use.

Regarding the task of retrieval, CI applications should integrate an internal search engine to search the database for adding *precision* or the capacity to find exactly what CI users want both in terms of information and intelligence products. Browsing is another interesting process that consists of scanning an information neighborhood, for instance, examining all the documents relating to an industry, or a given company, or a particular topic.

Analysis of Information

Analysis is probably the most difficult process to automate because it is inherently a human activity. In the context of CI, analysis means using a number of techniques for sorting and comparing data and information, for deriving some interpretations, and for developing and testing hypotheses based on various assumptions. Synthesis is also necessary for that process to grasp the "big picture" as well as the details pertaining to competitors' behavior and their environment. In addition, analysis necessitates a fair amount of intention, judgment, and subjectivity. Walle (2001) suggests that CI is essentially a qualitative methodology and should integrate more social sciences and humanities tools because competition evolves in unpredictable ways. For this reason, CI professionals must, to some extent, develop a "sixth sense" to help them foresee what might happen in their industry. According to Westney and Ghoshal (1994), CI clients are frequently dissatisfied with the limited amount of analysis produced by analysts who are often overwhelmed with collecting and organizing information. Analyzing competitors' strategies or competitive forces is not grounded in one specific academic discipline such as political science or economics. Although rooted in military strategy (Cronin, 2000), such analysis is indeed interdisciplinary, complex, and does not rely on well-established techniques. Given the level of expertise and judgment and the intense manipulation of data required for good analysis, the use of information technology is limited in its contribution, which mainly consists of providing assistance in organizing data and information. CI is similar to statistics in the sense that, although technology is useful for generating useful data, their interpretation requires a qualitative analysis with a human element. This qualitative appreciation is key for converting information into intelligence. In fact, all of the previous processes are aimed at creating the best conditions for accurate analysis.

Surveys conducted by SCIP reveal that their members use a number of CI tools for analyzing information: competitor profiles, financial analysis, SWOT analysis, scenario development, win/loss analysis, war gaming, conjoint analysis, and simulation/modeling (Powell and Allgaier, 1998). Other techniques such as benchmarking and gap analysis, core competencies, patent citation analysis, and value chain analysis have been reviewed by Sandman (2000). Newer sophisticated techniques are constantly being developed (Bergeron and Hiller, 2002) and can integrate marketing issues (Bulger, 2001) or data-mining techniques (Marín-Llanes et al., 2001). Ideally, CI software applications should be helpful for conducting various types of analysis, and should make CI users aware of techniques that might be useful for them.

We identified four potential processes related to the task of analyzing. *Variety of CI analytical techniques* refers to providing more than one technique for extracting meaning from information. It implies offering a choice of different analytical approaches. For instance, war gaming and scenario development are related techniques, whereas SWOT analysis and Porter's Five Forces are also complementary. Considering the purpose of each technique, the application could offer or recommend options to the user in relation to the problem at hand. Analytical techniques contribute to *noise reduction* and add *precision*. Offering a variety of techniques brings *adaptability* and the value of *closeness to the problem*. The

Level of analysis refers to the extent to which information is processed. For example, data on financial performance could be entered in the system and some financial analysis involving data correlation could be calculated. This functionality is similar to the mission of artificial intelligence and expert systems. At a minimal level, a CI system should give pointers to the users: if a certain type of analysis is required such as scenario development for a company *X,* given the list of competitors, it could generate automatically a number of key scenarios (e.g., merger, acquisition, partnership) and each would suggest questions to expand analytical thinking. *Level of analysis* addresses the need for *quality* and the value *comprehensiveness* by ensuring complete coverage of a particular analytical technique and by helping the user of the CI system to consider all the dimensions of the technique.

The next process is *Synthesis of information.* The ability of a system to summarize an article or report can free analysts to spend more time refining their analysis, and with recent improvements in automatic text summarization, it is realistic to expect this function in a CI application. In reducing the potential for information overload, such synthesis would support the user criterion of *noise reduction* and facilitate the value of *intellectual access.*

The last value-added dimension in this category, *Recommendations for action,* refers to intelligence that is analyzed to such an extent that it leads to decision making and actions. This can be seen as the highest level of value-added information as well as the final outcome of analysis. Again, it might take the form of pointers—for example, "given the strengths and weaknesses of scenarios A, B, and C identified previously ... the following things need to be considered for final recommendations" or "... these basic concerns should be taken into account by decision makers." On the other hand, if the results of analysis are too thin, the recommendation could be to acquire additional information that would support a valid decision. This type of function is linked to *quality* in terms of user criterion and would add the value of *validity* because the system would give signals about the extent to which the information presented can be considered sound and sufficient for appropriate decision making.

Development of CI Products

Regarding the design of specific CI products, it is essential to have an application that can handle various formats such as text, tables, graphs, pie charts, photographs, drawings, or even multimedia files with sound, in order to convey intelligence in the many ways CI requires. Given the current state of technology, the idea that CI outputs should be articulated strictly in text formats is passé. The issue here is the capability of a system to aggregate—or to put various types of information together in a comprehensive way in order to present the "big picture" in the most appropriate formats. CI products encompass many forms of reporting intelligence: newsletters, quarterly and annual reports on competitor profiles, news alerts in text format, news broadcasts (multimedia files), special projects reports, and so forth.

The criterion, *Variety of formats for viewing CI products,* deals with the capability to offer a number of formats by which CI clients can view the intelligence. This may include offering templates for the range of products that are needed on a regular basis, such as newsletters or competitor profiles. For the system user, this feature is represented by the user criterion, *ease of use*. The value criterion of *formatting* is obtained here because it becomes possible to highlight some sections of intelligence in a way that facilitates their scanning and understanding.

Effectiveness of formats refers to offering the formats that are particularly effective for presenting intelligence. As Westney and Ghoshal (1994) argue, effective presentation of data can enhance its impact and, conversely, ineffective presentation can induce inappropriate interpretation. A software application could suggest options in relation to the type of data or information to be presented. As mentioned before, the system should offer *adaptability* and *quality*, and this particular process would meet the values *simplicity*, in order to present the most clear data and information, and *validity*, for the soundness and appropriateness of the format.

Flexibility for adapting CI products requires a system capable of converting one format into another, according to user requirements. Ideally, the application should permit a number of processes—for example, that the text content in tables can be easily converted into paragraphs and vice-versa; that the numerical data could be converted either to graphs, histograms, or pie charts; and customizability, allowing users to pick and choose the specific pieces of intelligence to be included in the final product. For the system user, this feature again means *adaptability*, and the value *flexibility* is added.

Distribution of CI Products

The distribution of intelligence products finishes up the CI cycle and constitutes a crucial step because it relates to dissemination of CI products to the communities of clients identified beforehand. Of course, the final CI product has no value unless it is distributed. Paradoxically, senior managers are often reluctant to encourage a wide distribution of CI products, especially if they represent highly value-added information. This is often a major frustration of CI analysts (Westney and Ghoshal, 1994). The dissemination of the results also changes the CI requirements of the client community, thus beginning the CI cycle over again. The need for a good balance between written, oral, and electronic modes of delivery is a central issue here. The most sophisticated and detailed report will be useless if most decision makers do not appreciate reading long documents. It might be more appropriate to organize briefings and oral presentations. To date, no software application can offer all modes of distribution. However, an application should support some of them. The first criterion, *Capacity for distributing CI products,* refers mainly to the capability of a system to forward electronic CI products to clients by e-mail or through the intranet, or even through a voice-messaging system. The value here is *physical accessibility* because this facilitates the use of all CI outputs.

The next process, *Identification of potential CI consumers,* suggests that the system should help to identify the individual(s) who will benefit from the intelligence. Given the nature and focus of particular CI products, additional consumers who are not members of the main communities of CI clients are likely to be interested in specific outputs. For example, if the whole cycle generates a report on a corporate strategy focusing on research and development, the R & D unit will also benefit from the results. This means that before disseminating the report, the software application would support a careful examination of all the receivers of intelligence. Such a function would address the criterion *adaptability* and the value *closeness to the problem,* to make sure that specific intelligence needs are met.

Other Evaluation Criteria

As is the case for any software application, it is essential to assess the way an average user will employ a CI system from a user-friendly point of view. We listed six criteria dealing with several dimensions. The first three are: *Ease of use of the interface,* referring to how easy it is to use the menu, if one is provided, and to understand the commands required for the software; the *Usefulness of help facility,* or the help function; and *Requirement of technical expertise* in order to be able to use the application. These three criteria address the notion of *ease of use* and the value *interfacing* because they all facilitate use of a CI system by enabling the user to more easily understand all the system features and their potential. *Navigation features* refers to the engineering that allows users to move around easily within the various functions of the application and corresponds to the value *browsing.* An application that is difficult to navigate is much less likely to be used to its fullest capabilities. Additionally, logical navigation within a system can help users clarify their CI needs and practices. This potential serendipity is important given the iterative dimension of CI and the need to constantly modify, adapt, and improve the CI cycle. *Capability for changing display* and *Software compatibility* are connected to the criteria of *adaptability* and *flexibility.*

Additional Considerations

The general evaluation criteria presented here are by no means comprehensive, but are merely examples of other types of system features that contribute to the value of a software application. Many other evaluation criteria could be added, for example the cost of training required or the installation time. An extensive body of literature presents and discusses evaluation criteria of generic software. Thus, these general criteria will not be demonstrated in Chapter 5. However, when purchasing software it is important to keep in mind the relevance of other criteria beyond those that measure the software's ability to fulfill its stated purpose. Two other user criteria mentioned by Taylor that are also not raised here are time and cost saving. The evaluation of the money and time that an organization would save by using a CI application cannot be properly determined without conducting a significant study of the impact on users. Although these are important value-added aspects, their assessment would necessitate experiments, surveys, or case studies. An evaluation using the 32 criteria presented in this chapter will be demonstrated in Chapter 5. These 32 criteria, based on the value-added process of CI, were developed to provide a useful method for users to determine whether a CI software package will meet their competitive intelligence needs.

In the next chapter, we discuss the nature of the CI software market, present a typology of CI technology, and describe several CI software applications that are available today.

CHAPTER 4

Overview of Competitive Intelligence Software Applications and Related Products

Interest in the CI function has significantly increased within the North American business community since the 1980s. As a result, a number of resources and tools to support its function have emerged. These include CI consulting companies, information services, software packages, and CI training courses. To date, there is no definitive data about the existing market for CI-related software and services, but conservative estimates suggest that it is in the range of $100–$200 million (US$) and growing (Fleisher and Blenkhorn, 2001), and the market for BI and CI software was estimated to be $148 billion by Survey.com (cited by Fuld & Co., 2001). According to the most recent survey by Fuld & Co. (2002) conducted in 2000, the demand for CI products is high, with 72 percent of respondents indicating that they were planning to develop or purchase some type of CI tool.

Looking closely at the products and services included in this market, it becomes obvious that many firms are trying to capitalize on the popularity of CI to increase sales of their products. This is particularly true of software designers whose products—although not specifically designed or tailored to the needs of CI—can be used to support the process. The range of software products currently offered on the market to support CI is broad and includes customized search engines, alert services, commercial online databases, data mining and data warehousing applications, and general database solutions. The fact that so many products are labeled CI is indicative of the ambiguity regarding the scope and the nature of the CI process.

Where does CI start and where does it end? Of the 170 potential CI software packages identified by Fuld & Co. in 2000, the *Intelligence Software Report* concluded that the majority of applications do not perform CI at all, and only 12 packages were assessed. For the *2002*

Intelligence Software Report, Fuld & Co. reviewed 13 packages in depth, suggesting that the number of applications having sufficient CI functionality remains small. The "CI Resource Index" (http://www.bidigital.com/ci) developed and maintained by CISeek.com lists more than 289 potential CI software applications, but many of these products have tenuous connections to the CI process as a whole. Internet search tools, information portals, business intelligence tools, knowledge management software applications, intranet solutions, and online CI services are listed alongside CI software packages without much differentiation. Developing and maintaining a list of CI-related applications is a challenge for a number of reasons. Many products are introduced to the market but have very short commercial lives. Our examination of the CI Resource Index illustrates this dilemma—the links to several applications listed are no longer valid. The vast majority of CI products found on the list fall into the general category of Internet search tools and, more specifically, tools for monitoring information sources on the Web, presupposing that CI requires an information-searching activity in general, and Web searching in particular. Presenting these tools as CI software is somewhat legitimate and is consistent with the broad definitions of CI systems that can be found in the literature (Bergeron and Hiller, 2002; Hohhof, 1994; 2000). Many of these search tools were designed and in use long before the advent of the CI software products we will be discussing here, and they are truly useful in the context of CI. Thus these types of software will continue to be categorized as CI products. However, given recent developments with CI applications, it is important to differentiate more critically between the products that perform the CI process more comprehensively from other products that support only a portion of the CI cycle. Based on the descriptions provided by manufacturers, we found that fewer than 10 percent of the products listed in the CI Resource Index could be considered bonafide CI software applications. This problem is compounded by the fact that some CI-related activities occur in other business processes such as Business Intelligence (BI) and Knowledge Management (KM). According to Fuld & Co. (2002), BI tools focus mainly on data mining and quantitative analysis of corporate data, and have little to no value for CI purposes, KM technologies seek mainly to support knowledge sharing and collaborative work (Bouthillier and Shearer, 2002) and employ applications such as information portals and intranet solutions. Although CI is increasingly linked to KM (Barclay and Kaye, 2000; Breeding, 2000; Davenport and Hall, 2002), KM technologies do not usually address the specific nature of the CI cycle.

The purpose of this chapter is to give an overview of the various applications that support the CI cycle and to help readers differentiate the products that have a sophisticated CI functionality from those that are useful only for related tasks. To begin, the products have been categorized and mapped to the CI steps performed. In our view, a CI software application is one that has been designed to support the performance of several key steps in the CI process. Thus, for a product to be considered a CI software package here, we require that it meet a set of criteria. The basic selection criteria are outlined in detail in this chapter, along with brief descriptions of the six software packages that meet these criteria.

That this is a highly volatile field cannot be stressed enough. CI software applications disappear, new ones appear, and new versions of existing packages are offered with increasing frequency. For this reason, the software discussed here and in Chapter 5 serve merely to illustrate the performance of "typical" CI software applications, rather than as definitive descriptions and evaluations of specific software packages. By the time you read this, the software described here most likely will have changed or even disappeared. The real and lasting value of this typology of products and the evaluation criteria presented in Chapter 5 is the usefulness in gaining a better understanding of the ability of software in general to perform the various tasks involved in the CI process, regardless of the rate at which the products metamorphose.

A Typology of Technologies

CI practitioners—the main consumers of CI software products—are typically not trained in evaluating information technology and, thus, may have a difficult time in assessing the value of the various products, or even distinguishing them from other types of applications such as database management systems, e-business applications, or sophisticated search engines. A 1997 survey conducted by Fuld & Co. confirms this. When respondents were asked to identify computer-based intelligence applications, they often named information sharing and storage software packages such as Microsoft

Access, Lotus Notes, and Intranets—none of which, at that time, would have been considered intelligence applications (Fuld & Co., 1998). The preliminary results of a survey among French CI practitioners (Favier, 2002) reveal that traditional software packages, such as word processing, spreadsheets, and those that perform basic storage functions, are the most common types of software packages used in the context of CI. Does that mean that these packages are CI products? Our answer is no; otherwise, anything is a CI product.

The fact that CI is not a well-defined concept with definitive boundaries limits practitioners' ability to critically evaluate software applications. As in any other field, a quick rise in popularity is often accompanied by products and services endeavoring to capitalize on the popularity. Some software manufacturers, wishing to profit from this market, make false claims about their products' capabilities (Miller, 1999). With no commonly accepted methods for evaluating CI products, practitioners are particularly vulnerable to these false claims. Having no mechanisms to evaluate CI software independently, practitioners are left to rely on others' assessments. Since 1998, Fuld & Co. has published several evaluation reports on CI software packages. These valuable reports provide a basic description of the strengths and weaknesses of the various software packages. However, we feel that a widely available set of evaluation criteria based on a comprehensive theoretical model of CI is also needed to enable practitioners to understand the origins of the criteria, critique them, and customize them to meet the needs of their own organizations.

Not surprisingly, CI practitioners are generally dissatisfied with the quality of the "commercial off-the-shelf" (COTS) CI software packages available. A COTS software application is a product developed externally (as opposed to in-house) and delivered in executable format (as opposed to source-code format). A 1997 survey of 40 businesses, conducted by Fuld & Co. in conjunction with SCIP, found that respondents rated their CI software applications (some were CI-specific and some were general business application systems) as inadequate in many areas, such as acquiring information, disseminating results, and, most of all, in performing analysis (Fuld & Co., 1998). The situation is not unique to CI software products, and many organizations struggle with selecting an appropriate product for use in their systems, regardless of function.

Businesses are also using other types of software to facilitate the process of CI. Some organizations choose to implement more general software systems, such as knowledge management or database management systems, rather than to employ a system specifically designed for CI. Intranets and Lotus Notes have been, and continue to be, two of the most popular applications used for CI (Fuld & Co., 1997; Johnson, 1999). One informal survey conducted in 1999 found that many CI practitioners had built systems of their own to aid in the competitive intelligence process, despite the fact that these systems tended to be much more costly than the COTS software available for CI (Johnson, 1999).

However, the use of COTS software continues to rise for both governments and private industry, especially to facilitate critical business systems (Albert and Brownsword, 2002). Although the users do not have access to the source code, they choose COTS software for some very simple reasons: they are considered to be much more cost-effective than software developed in-house, which often requires lengthy development cycles and a substantial budget, and, because COTS products are developed in the commercial marketplace, they are thought to have increased capability, reliability, and functionality for the end-user over what would be available from custom-built software.

The variety of products that have been associated with CI can be categorized into a typology (Table 4.1). Because technology develops at such a rapid pace and software designs can evolve in many directions, it is almost impossible to develop an exhaustive typology. At the moment, one of the major trends in software development is convergence; that is, to create systems that can accomplish numerous functions and serve many purposes. The typology presented here lists 13 basic types of products that can handle structured or unstructured information. The typology was designed to indicate the range of the technological devices that can be found on the market for business/CI applications. Each technology supports some aspects of information retrieval and management.

Some of the technologies listed in Table 4.1 are well established software systems, such as Web searching and document management applications. However, over the last few years, several new technologies have emerged and become commonplace, including Profiling or Push Technology, Filtering or Intelligent Agent Technology, Analyzing and Structuring Technology, Text Discovering, BI and E-Business Applications, and Multipurpose Portals. Push technology is valued because it saves time by alerting users about

Table 4.1 Typology of Technologies Associated with CI

Technology	Description	Examples of Software Name (Company)
1. Profiling or Push Technology	Provides automatically at regular intervals or real-time data or text from multiple sources (Internet and/or intranet) based on interest profiles or predetermined queries; can look for changes and alert user.	Back Web e-Accelerator (BackWeb) Verity Profiler Kit (Verity Inc.)
2. Filtering or Intelligent Agent Technology	Monitors Web sites, documents, and e-mail messages to filter information according to particular preferences; can learn user preferences; can highlight the most important part automatically; can provide text summary; can prioritize, delete, or forward information automatically.	Copernic Enterprise Search (Copernic) Copernic Agent Pro (Copernic)
3. Web Searching	Customized search engines (Web crawlers or meta-crawlers) to launch queries automatically in various databases or on various search engines.	Deep Query Manager/LexiBot (Bright Planet) BullsEye (Intelliseek) Copernic Agent Basic/Personal (Copernic) Digout4U (Arisem)
4. Text Mining	Conducts higher-level text searching through linguistic patterning. Involves language recognition technology, word dictionaries with links between semantic concepts. Useful for more precise information retrieval.	LexiQuest (Lexiquest)
5. Text Summarizing	Pinpoints key concepts and extracts relevant sentences, resulting in a summary of a larger document.	Copernic Summarizer (Copernic)
6. Text Discovering	Extracts concepts in textual information and maps out the relationships between them.	Semiomap (Semio Corporation)
7. Groupware	Encompasses several capabilities in one software application including messaging,	Lotus Domino (IBM) SunForum

	calendaring, e-mail, workflow, and centralized database.	(SunMicrosystems)
8. Document and Content Management	Encompasses several technology types into one software application including the storage of information in its original document format and capabilities of relational database, facilitating the identification of relevant information by searching a large volume of structured and unstructured information.	PowerDocs/CyberDocs (Hummingbird)
9. Text Analyzing and Structuring	Includes several types of technology in one software application for information acquisition, categorization, and organization, as well as analysis and formatting of final products. Can be used to develop taxonomies.	Intelligent Miner for Text (IBM)
10. Multipurpose Portals	Integrates corporate intranets (service hubs of mail, news, information) to provide access to internal and external sources; works as a platform, with groupware, automatic information retrieval, classification, and monitoring software.	OpenPortal4U (Arisem) Portal-in-a-box (Autonomy) Corporate Portal (Plumtree)
11. Business Intelligence and E-Business Applications	Integrates e-commerce, CRM (customer relationship management), and ERP (enterprise resource planning) solutions as well as the management of various processes (human resources, budgeting, accounting, supply chain). Helps to analyze data on customers and suppliers.	Companies such as Cognos, SAP, or Peoplesoft offer a wide range of this type of solution
12. Analyzing and Reporting Data	Extracts data, searches patterns, slices, dices, drills down to find meaning, and allows various reporting options.	Powerplay/Impromptu /DecisionStream (Cognos) BusinessObjects (Business Objects)
13. Information Services and Vendors	Provides access to information sources based on subscription, usually offers push technology, can provide features for presenting and distribution reports.	Includes Dialog, Factiva, Lexis, OneSource

new information when it is released on the Web. This technology, however, is not useful for retrieving information that is already released or existing and that is hidden in Web sites. Intelligent agents address this last dimension and have attracted much attention over the last few years (Abushar and Hirata, 2002; Desouza, 2001). They are valued for their ability to automatically locate documents on the basis of user preferences. The intention behind intelligent agents is to monitor the information environment and to identify relevant documents on behalf of the user. Therefore, they are helpful in saving time, but their main value is in retrieving quality information based on the user's definition of relevance.

Search engine technology is also receiving a great deal of attention recently (Chen et al., 2002). Developers are creating a new generation of Web search applications that offer more sophisticated indexing, querying, ranking, and clustering options than do current "mainstream" search engines such as AltaVista and Google. Many of these new search tools address the issue of quantity as well as quality, guaranteeing that a large number of documents matching a given query will be retrieved, and presenting the results in a highly structured order based on relevance.

The text mining/summarizing/discovering technologies presented in Table 4.1 also address the activity of information retrieval, while offering some level of analysis. They examine not only the subject-relatedness of texts as revealed by keywords found in titles and elsewhere, but also the concepts and linguistic patterns in the body of the text in order to extract significant parts or establish relationships between concepts. Groupware, document and content management, analyzing and structuring text software, and multipurpose portals offer various approaches to storing, organizing, and disseminating information. They create databases and make their content available to various groups of users. BI and E-Business applications as well as analyzing-and-reporting software seek to manipulate and analyze in-house corporate data. Their contribution to the CI function is debatable, depending on how broad the scope of CI is considered to be. In the broad sense, it can be argued that gaining a greater understanding of customers, suppliers, or sales patterns is an important prerequisite to properly understanding one's competitors. And finally, information vendors are included in the typology because they also support information retrieval through the use of innovative technology. Many of these vendors employ integrated technology that can create sophisticated information products such as reports, graphs, and diagrams based on information that has been retrieved in their databases, and disseminate their products via various channels including e-mail. Some vendors have also added push technology features in order to alert subscribers to relevant information that is added to their databases.

Although the typology presented is representative of the major trends existing in the marketplace, it has its limitations. The rapid rate of evolution and convergence of technology means that no typology can be comprehensive. Similarly, the names of applications and of companies selling these applications are constantly changing. Thus, we selected only software applications that have been available for a number of years as examples for our typology. This classification is not entirely satisfactory because we can find products that combine a number of functions. An application such as "WebExpress," produced by Convera (formerly RetrievalWare, from Excalibur Technologies), is a good example. This is a search tool that integrates various features (e.g., Concept Search and Adaptive Pattern Recognition Processing) to collect, monitor, and index documents and that compensates for misspellings and typos, which often prevent the retrieval of relevant documents. It is also possible that some of the examples provided in Table 4.1 may be discontinued or repackaged under a new label in the near future due to mergers of software companies or to the addition of new features.

What value do these software applications have for the CI process? The lack of a widely accepted definition of CI has undoubtedly influenced the incorrect identification of products as "CI software." No standards exist regarding the terminology used for the advertising of these products and in many cases vendors use CI and/or BI as selling points. The fact is that CI requires a number of activities (e.g., acquisition, storage, and distribution of information), most of which can be performed adequately with existing desktop software involving a suite of applications (e.g., word processing, presentations, spreadsheet, e-mail). Even though it would be safe to say that none of the products presented in Table 4.1 were designed specifically for CI, they can certainly contribute to many of the activities involved in CI. The technologies listed in Table 4.1 have been mapped to the step in the CI process that corresponds with its function (Table 4.2).

For the most part, these technologies prove to be useful for one or two steps in the CI process, mainly the acquisition function, or the organizing and storing function. This is not surprising, as technology

Table 4.2 Technologies Associated with CI and Their Corresponding CI Processes

Competitive Intelligence Process	Technology
Identification of CI needs	None
Acquisition of competitive information	Profiling/push technology
	Filtering/intelligent agent technology
	Web searching
	Information services/vendors
Organization, storage, and retrieval	Document and content management
	Text discovering
	Groupware
	Multipurpose portals
	Text analyzing and structuring
	Analyzing and reporting data
	BI and e-business applications
Analysis of information	Text summarizing
	Text analyzing and structuring
	Analyzing and reporting data
Development of CI products	Text summarizing
	Text analyzing and structuring
	Analyzing and reporting data
	Information services/vendors
Distribution of CI products	Groupware
	Multipurpose portals
	Information services/vendors

has been used to facilitate both of these functions for a relatively long period of time. The more well-established technologies, such as Web Search Engines, Document and Content Management, and Reporting

Tools, tend to perform the acquisition, organization, and storage; development of intelligence products; and distribution of intelligence functions. As technology advances, we are beginning to see new applications designed to perform more advanced functions. However, within the realm of CI software, the technology still falls short of what are typically called expert systems. The technology addresses the analysis process through categorizing information, rather than integrating a knowledge base. Nevertheless, we are seeing a definite shift toward intelligence systems as applications begin to perform a greater number of automated tasks such as filtering, indexing, and categorizing.

The fact that no one application performs the entire CI process does not diminish the possible contribution of the various available applications to information-related activities within an organization. However, it is important to draw a distinction between software applications that can be used to facilitate one or two steps in the CI process and those that attempt to facilitate a complete CI function. Most individual steps in the CI cycle can be effectively conducted using basic technology: competitive information can be efficiently acquired through e-mail, search engines, and information services (though probably not completely); information can be organized and stored using database management applications (with the help of the CI practitioner); CI products are created through various reporting tools (word processing, spreadsheets, presentation tools); and, intelligence can be distributed through intranets and e-mail systems. In fact, technology can efficiently perform all the required activities in CI except one: the jury is still out as to whether the analysis function of CI can be conducted or facilitated to any great degree by technology. Clearly, in order to more completely perform CI, there is a need—and a trend—to combine several of these technologies into one platform. This is precisely what the more recently introduced CI software applications have attempted to do (Fuld & Co., 2002).

One of the major distinctions to be made when evaluating CI software applications is between COTS products and software that performs CI, but is owned and housed externally. COTS products are purchased from a vendor and integrated into a company's own environment, whereas, on the other hand, companies can use an application service provider (ASP) for their CI needs. An ASP is a company that offers access over the Internet to applications and related services that would otherwise have to be located on the user's own personal or enterprise computer system. The final category in our typology, "information services/vendors," are ASPs rather than COTS. The advantages of ASPs are that no space is required on the user's hard drive, they require little or no integration time, and there is no need for in-house maintenance. However, ASPs have inherent security risks that discourage most companies from using them as complete CI solutions. Companies will often use ASPs to acquire information, but they are reluctant to store the competitive intelligence outcome externally.

Identifying CI Technology

There are some simple selection criteria that practitioners can use to eliminate software packages before beginning the time-consuming process of evaluating them all. First of all, the software application should perform three or four steps in the CI cycle, rather than just one or two steps. Within the CI process are several steps that take higher precedence than others. The identification of intelligence needs is a very important step that precedes the acquisition of information. CI differs from other intelligence processes in that the information and intelligence needs are specific to the variables affecting the ability of ones' competitors to remain competitive. Therefore, one criterion for selecting CI software to be evaluated is its focus toward the specific information needs of CI. BI and e-business applications, for example, are used to conduct analysis of customers and suppliers, but do not contain competitor-specific information, and therefore cannot be considered CI software. Although many of the technologies listed in Table 4.2 could potentially be tailored to the specific needs of CI in a COTS software product, most are not. Several of the other technologies listed are very general and may be used in any intelligence process. The Web searching or text mining types are not designed to search for competitor information, but can be used to search for any type of information as instructed by the user.

A second highly important step in CI is the analysis function, which involves various possible levels of analysis. Basic analysis involves linking, synthesis, and comparison of disparate pieces of information. At its higher level, analysis involves hypothesis and inference based on expert knowledge. Analysis is a requirement for CI and any CI software should perform or should help the user to achieve some level of analysis. Thus, a second criterion for selecting CI software for evaluation is that the software performs at least some basic level of analysis.

The market for CI software has become more sophisticated of late. In their 2002 report, *Intelligence Software: The Global Evolution*, Fuld & Co., observed an overall improvement in the technological solutions available for competitive intelligence. New technologies are being implemented to facilitate the various steps in the CI cycle, and these technologies are being combined into single systems that more closely resemble the complete CI process.

As discussed, three important selection criteria must be considered when distinguishing CI software from other types of software, regardless of how that software is marketed:

1. The software must perform more than two (preferably four or five) value-added processes similar to those outlined in the CI cycle.

2. These value-added processes must include identifying intelligence needs that are tailored specifically to CI.

3. The software must perform some level of analysis.

In an attempt to identify the available CI software packages, we conducted an Internet search using the terminology "competitive intelligence software" and reviewed the resource lists available through several CI related organizations (CI Resource Index, 2002; Fuld & Co., 2002; SCIP, 2002). On the basis of the steps involved in the CI cycle, we were able to identify six off-the-shelf software packages (these can be installed on personal computers or on a company's LAN) designed to provide CI practitioners with a comprehensive technological solution. Only off-the-shelf-packages were included because, as discussed previously, the use of their Web-based counterparts raises a number of security concerns for those dealing with potentially sensitive information. We are likely to see a growing number of Web-based CI applications as the security issues are addressed; however, at this time we cannot confidently recommend the use of such products.

Our selection criteria differ from those used by Fuld & Co. (2002). In its most recent study, the firm evaluated both CI-specific packages (covering several steps of the CI cycle) and CI-related applications (dealing with only one or two steps of the CI cycle). Thus, the 13 applications chosen by Fuld & Co. vary considerably and include tools that have very different functionalities and prices, such as Web search engines (for instance, C-4-U Scout, which can be downloaded for free), text mining (for instance, TextAnalyst 2.0, which can cost $1,290 per user), and client-server applications (for instance, ClearResearch Suite, which can cost from $150,000 to $200,000). Fuld's approach for selecting CI packages indicates the prevailing inclusive view of what constitutes a CI product. Our goal here, however, was to select a limited number of the most comprehensive software products in order to demonstrate a framework for comparing and evaluating functionalities.

Table 4.3 contains a list of the six applications that meet our selection criteria. For each application, the table presents the name of the manufacturer and contact information, as well as the specific references made to the CI capability of the software. Interestingly, all of the applications that fulfilled our criteria and are presented here were also identified by Fuld & Co. (2002) with the exception of Viva Intelligence Portal.

As illustrated, each application describes itself specifically as a CI solution, but not necessarily exclusively so. Many of these packages claim to perform business intelligence, market analysis, or knowledge management as well as CI. An application such as Viva Intelligence Portal, designed in Finland, is advertised as a BI as well as a CI solution. It is worth mentioning that in Finland (and Europe in general), BI is thought to be synonymous to the concept of CI in the United States and Canada, where BI does not always include analysis of competitors.

The following section contains the basic product descriptions of software applications as provided by the companies in promotional material.

CI Software Products Overview

Based on product descriptions provided by their manufacturers, the basic features of the six applications identified in Table 4.3 are described in the following section.

Table 4.3 Commercial Off-the-Shelf Competitive Intelligence Software Applications

Name	Manufacturer	Contact Info	Self-Description
Knowledge. Works	Cipher Systems LLC Head Office: Glastonbury, CT U.S.	E-mail: b.aker@cipher-sys.com Web site: www.cipher-sys.com	Software for Competitive Intelligence
Market Signal Analyser	Docere Intelligence Head Office: Stockholm, Sweden	E-mail: info@docereusa.com Web site: www.docereintelligence .com	A comprehensive software that facilitates expert analysis of Competitive Intelligence and Market Analysis
Strategy!	Strategy Software, Inc. Head Office: Mill Creek, WA U.S.	E-mail: sales@strategy.cc Web site: www.strategy-software.com	Competitor Information Management System
Viva Intelligence Portal	Viva Business Intelligence Head Office: Helsinki, Finland	E-mail: info@vivaintelligence.com Web site: www.vivaintelligence.com	A user-friendly Web-based enterprise-wide solution that provides "one window" to all relevant Competitive Intelligence (CI) information that can be structured and classified according to corporate/user specific needs
Wincite	Wincite Systems LLC Head Office: Chicago, IL U.S.	E-mail: lgraff@wincitesystems.com Web site: www.wincite.com	Management Intelligence Portal, used for CI/BI/KM
Wisdom Builder	WisdomBuilder LLC Head Office: Columbia, MD, U.S.	E-mail: info@wisdombuilder.com Web site: www.wisdombuilder.com	A complete, end-to-end analytical tool focusing on investigative analysis and reporting

Knowledge.Works

The manufacturer of Knowledge.Works, Cipher Systems, was established in 1996 and is located in the United States. According to *Company Briefs*, the company had sales of $3 million in 2000, as opposed to $1.5 million in 1997 (Gale Group, 2002). These are estimates; the company is privately owned and does not release financial reports publicly. The company offers, in addition to CI software applications, various services such as a Consulting Center and a Technology & Education Center. Peter McKenney, the co-founder and chief executive officer, and Brooke Aker, the marketing and sales manager, are both well-known CI experts and have presented at many CI-related conferences. Knowledge.Works was ranked the number one application by Fuld & Co. in 2000, and, in its most recent report (Fuld & Co., 2002), even though no total final ranking is provided (an assessment of strengths and weaknesses for each application is given instead), Knowledge.Works received high marks for planning CI activities and collecting information. The product, specifically designed for CI, is marketed primarily to CI practitioners, and the promotional literature stresses the time and cost savings as a key value added by the product. A description of the product is available on the company Web site (http://www.cipher-sys.com/ website.nsf/Products?OpenPage).

Knowledge.Works can work with Microsoft Exchange/Outlook or Lotus Notes. It is described as "a file cabinet to store all sorts of information about competitors. Inside the file cabinet are automation features to categorize, index, search, alert, monitor, and subscribe to information for delivery to your e-mail, as a portal, or as a private intranet site." According to the manufacturer, the application offers "facilities to summarize text; to publish to the corporate intranet or portal; and to find, analyze, visualize, and navigate through the vast number of competitor puzzle pieces." The information might come from news vendors, the Web, or internal people.

Knowledge.Works integrates various other software applications that can be added based on users' needs. A Text Summarizer "allows users to reduce the amount of text to be read among any group of documents chosen" and "is particularly helpful in the creation of summaries of the filtered daily news"—offering a means to "extract the topical golden nuggets hidden within the database of competitive information." The Extended Search is a tool to facilitate the search of all available information both inside and outside the organization. According to the manufacturer, "results are compiled from the Internet and your internal storage areas, duplicates are removed, and a rank-order list is presented." In that sense, the application "aids in the automation and timeliness of searching for competitive information."

Another tool, Sametime, is designed to be used with the Lotus platform and can be added to allow the conduct of "real-time" sessions with colleagues instead of forwarding e-mail messages and waiting for responses. The promotional materials indicate that "workflow is aided by defining the questions you have about competitors and being clear about why it matters. Tasks are given to team members, follow-up is tracked, and reminders are e-mailed. Collecting new information from staff and trusted outsiders follows. Live interactive analysis can be done. Interpretation of the collected evidence results in answers being written. Managers who have the questions about competitors receive the answers from which they can issue action items to proactively outsmart and outmaneuver the competition." SharePoint, which can be integrated into the Microsoft platform, "indexes as well as finds and minds all the Internet and internal storage areas for your CI efforts." It is presented as having a feature for "alerting and routing on an individual basis." Finally, Learning Space "is used to create, manage, and distribute education opportunities in CI." Instructors and students can interact and retrieve information.

Market Signal Analyzer

Docere Intelligence Technology is a Swedish company. According to its Web site, it has been "considered as a leader in the field of CI since 1982" (http://www.docereintelligence.com/tech/technology2. htm). The managing director, Bobo af Ekenstam, is active in CI circles and in SCIP. Market Signal Analyzer was examined by Fuld & Co. (2002) and scored very high in the collection of information and for reporting tasks. The product is described as "a comprehensive software which facilitates expert analysis of Competitive Intelligence" that provides a "continuous lookout for market signals." According to the manufacturer, the application is designed "to identify, structure, analyze, and present market signals by focusing, collecting, structuring, and then analyzing qualitative information followed by the creation of reports." It is stated that "market signals come in many forms and, seen separately, they may mean little or nothing" and that Market Signal Analyzer can be used "to bring these signals together, view them in a wider context, and provide the overview needed to stay ahead of the competition." This represents the methodology on which Market Signal Analyzer is based.

Interestingly, Docere Intelligence explains the intelligence process that is covered by Market Signal Analyzer, identifying the following steps in its documentation:

- **Information Input**—Information from external sources is automatically loaded into the system and placed in a queue. Other information can be entered manually or e-mailed into the system by members of your organization.

- **Structuring**—Information is then analyzed and annotated. Next the information is categorized, making more detailed analysis possible through a matrix structure.

- **Analyzing**—The matrix makes it possible to view market signals from different perspectives and on an on-going basis. The matrix also makes it very easy to create a SWOT analysis. The matrix is three dimensional, using a time dimension in addition to the X and Y axis.

- **Presentation/Communication**—An effective way of presenting analyzed information to your organization is through an intranet. Using this facility, the Market Signal Analyzer can create and publish different reports. With less time spent on administration, there is more time for analysis!

By providing this information, Docere makes its definition of CI explicit suggesting that the application is designed to address the critical steps of the CI cycle.

Strategy!

Strategy! is a well-known product in CI quarters and is manufactured by Strategy Software Inc., located in the United States and founded in 1996. Strategy! president George Durtler has a diversified business background, having been a CEO for other companies (http://www.strategy-software.com). Strategy! is positioned by its manufacturer as an off-the-shelf "Competitor Information Management System." It is a database specifically designed to hold valuable information about competitors and other forces in the competitive environment. It scored very high in the Fuld & Co. review (2002) in the areas of primary source collection, analysis, and reporting. The

product is described in these terms: "an easy-to-use interface provides access to all competitive information in a straightforward
manner ... Strategy! was designed to include extensive customization ability to suit most company requirements, all without the need
for programming." According to the manufacturer, the application
offers the following features:

- More than 150 built-in reports can be selected to help to
  answer the most common questions that organizations ask.

- Product comparison reports can be generated very easily.

- It is possible to record where a summarized piece of information (Info Nuggets) came from, allowing any user to go back
  to the source and read/see/hear the original source when it is
  important.

- As a centralized repository for competitive information,
  Strategy! makes corporate knowledge available to the entire
  enterprise.

- To guarantee security, access is controlled on both user and
  user group levels. The administrator can control who can view
  information and who can make changes. Hybrid security
  models are also possible to restrict access to delicate areas of
  information. In addition, databases can be encrypted to pro-
  tect sensitive information on a laptop computer.

- Reports can be saved as HTML pages, Word documents, or
  Excel Spreadsheets.

- The user-configurable Menu and Toolbar should suit both
  occasional and power users: "ideal for occasional users who
  need fast information, and busy executives with no time to
  study a user's manual."

- The initial configuration of Strategy! covers a company's direct
  competitors and their products. Users may want to extend
  their "competitive awareness" to other competitive forces and

topics with advanced capabilities and advanced topics, allowing for a gradual understanding of the competition.

Viva Intelligence Portal

Viva Intelligence Portal is manufactured by Viva Business Intelligence, established in 1995 and located in Finland. Managing director Markko Vaarnas is very active in CI circles in this country, and has a degree in international business (http://www.vivaintelligence.com/eng/tech.asp?cat=70). Although Viva Intelligence Portal was not included in the 2002 Fuld & Co. CI software evaluation, it did meet our selection criteria. According to its manufacturer, the application "combines business information from external and internal sources, as well as content management tools, into an easy to use Web-browser interface." It is presented as a component of the organization's intranet and can work as the entry point for the organization's Business Intelligence network. "The Portal is built on a carefully planned information architecture that is tailored to the client organization's specific information needs." In addition, "the information content is structured into specific Business Intelligence modules that, together with the information architecture, provide a logical and easy way to process and distribute information."

The product's browser-based content management features are designed to facilitate easy information entry by virtually anyone in the organization. "In addition to being a simple system for administrators, content producers, and editors to work with, the structure of the Portal also makes information retrieval for the end-user extremely easy and accurate."

The application must be customized to meet a client's precise needs. "Basic setup typically consists of modules for handling news, market signals, company profiles, and analysis documents." The company claims that "external information sources and existing internal systems can also be integrated to the Viva Intelligence Portal."

According to the manufacturer's specifications, the basic modules include:

- **News Mill**—The most important news concerning the business environment is easily structured and distributed with the News Mill module.

- **Hot Signals Communicator**—Market signals and other "hot" information can easily be shared with the Hot Signals Communicator. It enables dynamic use of "front line" information from the organization's intelligence network.

- **Research & Analyses Library**—The Research & Analyses document database is used to store and share externally produced market analyses and in-house research reports or other related documents.

- **Profiler**—The Profiler is a highly customizable tool for compiling, distributing, and benchmarking key information on subjects of interest such as competitors, customers, countries, products, and so forth. The Profiler presents information in a concise, easily understandable manner and contains a wide set of features for viewing, comparing, and updating information.

- **Info Sources Directory**—The Info Source Directory is typically a directory of external information sources used by the company. By managing information sources from a centralized location, redundant use of often expensive sources can be avoided and information about the sources themselves, such as descriptions, costs, and contact persons, can be easily updated and distributed.

- **Personal Intelligence Service**—Different people within an organization have individual information needs. The Personal Intelligence Service can automatically update the user of new content matching his or her personal preferences, by e-mail or via the Portal itself.

Wincite

Wincite is owned by Wincite Systems LLC, founded in 1986 and located in the United States. The company reported $1.3 million in sales in 2000, down from $2 million in 1998 (Gale Group, *Company Briefs*, 2002). Wincite Systems LLC's president, Donald R. Smith, has extensive experience in the consulting business and worked for Price Waterhouse for 30 years. According to Fuld & Co. (2002), Wincite's strengths are in the areas of analysis and reporting. Wincite Systems

LLC launched a new version of Wincite in June 2002, with increased search capability, navigation features, and profile and benchmarking reporting options. Excerpts from the promotional materials available on the company Web site (http://www.wincite.com/WinciteWeb/ ProductsServices/wincitefeatures.htm) present the software as follows:

- Wincite is based on an underlying relational database, such as Microsoft SQL or Oracle that provides scalability to support thousands of users. The database is directly connected to Web intranet services using eWincite. The Wincite interface targets users who can use the system without any formal training beyond the skills of using a Web Browser.

- Efficiency of navigation to tens of thousands of information sources is a primary design objective of the system. The Home Page interface feature provides access to specific segments of the database that relate to users' areas of interests. An application can have any number of Home Pages, each tailored to the unique needs of a user group or individual. The "click and view" buttons in a screen trigger the display of internal files and Web pages in a browser window that is embedded in the screen. Users can view Microsoft Office files, charts, images, maps, and PDF files without leaving a Wincite screen. The Wincite screens have a number of navigation controls that support ease of access to needed information and the option to drill down to detailed supporting documents and files. The screen painter in Wincite supports the addition and modification of screens and fields by business analysts. The Painter can be viewed as a business analyst's workbench for developing a very broad variety of applications that integrate a centralized database with a network of users throughout the organization.

- Each field in a Wincite screen has an audit card identifying who updated the field, when, information sources, and priorities. Live links to Web sites provide a means of automatically showing current information. Using stock ticker symbols you can link to a number of valuable financial and news-oriented Web pages. A number of functions support a high level of productivity in populating and maintaining the application.

Text and objects can be copied and pasted or dragged and dropped into fields and buttons.

- The Wincite database can be searched from different perspectives, such as the contents of the fields in the database, the subjects in the database, which fields have changed, and the file or addresses that are linked in the application. Wincite is frequently integrated with a company's internal search tools, such as Microsoft's Index Server or Site Server. The results of the search are displayed in Wincite as a list of hits ordered by the degree they match the user's criteria. The hit list has a brief summary of each selected document or file and access to the full contents of the document or file. Integration of a number of Web search engines to a single screen lets you click a button and display the related list of hits.

- Profile reports provide a quick summary of topic-related information that can be viewed online, printed out, or downloaded to Microsoft Word. Customize Profile reports enable a user to select the fields to be included and the order of presentation, as well as customized headers and footers. When these reports are saved and run later, they will reflect the most current information in the database.

Wisdom Builder

Wisdom Builder is manufactured by Wisdom Builder LLC, located in the United States. This application also scored well in the Fuld & Co. 2002 evaluation in the areas of information collection and reporting. It is described by the manufacturer as a means to free people from the time-consuming activities of data organization and database queries, allowing them to focus on high level interpretation and strategic impact assessment. According to the promotional literature, it is an intuitively designed system geared to "minimize the learning curve and maximize results." Wisdom Builder is "a total solution for your analysis and research needs," freeing people from learning "a dozen complex new applications" (http://wisdombuilder.com/products. htm). Interestingly, Wisdom Builder is also presented as a KM application. An enterprise version connects the application into the

LAN-based database management systems (MS SQL Server, Oracle, and Sybase) and facilitates the sharing of knowledge within the organization.

Wisdom Builder is based on a set of four phases describing the analytical research process. First, research requirement assessment can be done with a self-organizing outline manager to create a cataloging structure based on how the information needs to be analyzed. "Requirements can be partitioned into separate databases for maximum flexibility, and supporting comments can be captured about each requirement, providing a history of activities and record of analyst actions."

Second, for the collection of information, Wisdom Builder accepts information from almost any media and can connect directly to an intranet server. It features multimedia data acquisition and handling abilities for managing large volumes of raw data coming from employee knowledge and experience, scanned documents, and electronic sources such as document files, image files, audio and video clips, and Web pages.

Third, knowledge mining and analysis is possible once the information has been captured. Based on one's personal dictionary of key terms, the filtering out of extraneous data and the extracting of relevant facts are accomplished. "Relationships between any of the seven standard items—research, requirements, people, organizations, places, events, and products—are easily created and tracked. Relationships are established simply by pointing and clicking or dragging and dropping items. Visual data representation lets you see relationships at a glance, allowing you to make decisions, deductions, and conclusions of the highest accuracy in the shortest period of time. The threads of relationships are graphically shown to reveal connections that might otherwise stay hidden. And the entire database can be navigated through these relationships." Items can be bookmarked for subsequent report creation. Finally, reporting is possible based on a full range of report creation and distribution through hard copy, e-mail, or publication on Web servers. "Reports can be assembled literally by pointing, highlighting, and dragging relevant information items to report folders, where they are packaged and converted into formatted intelligence documents. More than three dozen template reports address a variety of needs from standard list reports to profile reports, relationship reports, and custom sorted reports. Plus, they can be saved in standard PC file formats, including DOC, XLS, WKS, HTML, and more."

The product descriptions provided by the manufacturers of these software packages suggest that they address most steps of the CI process. All six packages approach the CI function as a process comprising a number of activities and incorporate a variety of technologies in order to facilitate more than one step in that process. Similarly, each package is tailored to the CI cycle by recognizing the unique intelligence needs of CI. In addition, the software packages all identify the analysis step as a central dimension of CI and, presumably, address this process in their technologies.

The companies behind all six products are privately owned (making it difficult to ascertain the full scope of their activities), relatively young firms, in business for less than 20 years—some for less than 10 years. All are run by executive officers with master's degrees in management and/or extensive experience in the business world.

It is clear that CI software must incorporate a variety of technologies in order to perform the range of activities required by the CI process. In particular, CI has unique information needs: the information must be acquired from a variety of sources; the information must be organized and stored; and, ultimately, the information must be transformed into intelligence through analysis. In Chapter 5, we present an evaluation of four of the six CI software applications described here. The packages are evaluated based on their ability to perform CI using the set of criteria presented in Chapter 3.

Evaluating Competitive Intelligence Software

Software evaluation is not a simple process and can be quite daunting, particularly for those who are not experts in software technology. Even for experienced evaluators, it is a time-consuming and detailed operation. As a result, technology users often give up and select off-the-shelf software packages based on their price, compatibility with database management systems, or the persuasiveness of the sales pitch rather than the ability of that software package to fulfill the purpose of the activity required.

The purpose of this chapter is to present a set of questions to evaluate CI software that is as straightforward and unambiguous as possible. The evaluation questions are grouped according to their related step in the CI process and will be used to evaluate four CI applications. To date, no well-established and comprehensive set of evaluation criteria for CI software applications has been published. It is our hope that by making these evaluation criteria available to the public, they will be discussed, critiqued, and refined within the larger CI community. Ideally, the criteria will be used by CI software purchasers to assess the strengths and weaknesses of CI applications, and, similarly, that they will be considered by software designers to improve the quality of CI software applications.

Our evaluation of four CI software packages is followed by a comparison of them based on their ability to fulfill the purpose of CI, as well as a discussion of the strengths and weaknesses of each. The comparison is not intended to assess the efficiency, effectiveness, usability, or acceptability of each package but, rather, to establish whether or not the selected CI software products involve a number of value-added processes that contribute to the metamorphosis of information into intelligence. Thus, no score or final ranking will be assigned to the products being evaluated. Instead, a simple yes or no answer is given to each of the evaluation questions, followed by a summary of the assessment of each major step of the CI cycle. At the end of the evaluation, the number of yes and no answers for each product is compiled.

As discussed earlier, our evaluation should not be used as a definitive assessment of the selected software packages, primarily because of modifications and upgrades that may have already occurred. We think of the evaluation as comparable to our photographing a landscape at a specific point in time: We have captured a moment, but not those changes in the landscape that are certain to follow. A value in this technique is in documenting a number of landmarks that may serve to help software providers and users understand in what areas existing products have a strong functionality, and in what areas there is room for improvement. However, we believe that the most important contribution of this project to the CI community is in the formulation of a comprehensive set of criteria that can be used to evaluate any CI software package. In the Appendix of the book, you will find a "Do-It-Yourself Evaluation Form for CI Software," which lists all of the evaluation questions. Keep in mind that the meaning and purpose of many of the evaluation questions on the form may not be clear to those who have not read this chapter and, indeed, previous chapters of the book.

An Evaluation Guide: Criteria and Questions

The evaluation criteria presented in Chapter 3, which were derived from the CI process, have been translated here into evaluation questions in keeping with current technology. As with the criteria, the questions target a software application's capability to perform the entire CI cycle and are categorized according to each step in the CI process. Table 5.1 shows the evaluation questions matched up with their corresponding criterion. The criteria and questions here reflect the current state of technological development and seek to examine what can be done automatically by an application, or whether the application facilitates the task allowing for the user to do it manually.

Methodology

Numerous software packages were identified for this evaluation through an examination of the information provided by the Society

Table 5.1   Evaluation Criteria and Evaluation Questions

Evaluation Criteria: Value-Added Processes	Evaluation Questions
I. Identification of CI needs	
1. Identification of main CI client communities	Does the application help to identify the main CI client communities?
2. Identification of CI topics	Does the application help to identify CI topics?
3. Translation of intelligence topics into specific information requirements	Does the application help to identify the pieces of information required to address the CI topics?
4. Identification of CI analytical techniques	Does the application help to identify CI analytical techniques to address the needs of the CI clients?
5. Capability to change CI topics and analytical techniques	Can the CI topics and analytical techniques be changed?
II. Acquisition of competitive information	
6. Identification of external information sources	Does the application help to identify external information sources?
7. Identification of internal information sources	Does the application help to identify internal information sources?
8. Identification of sources for specific topics	Does the application relate information sources with specific topics?
9. Monitoring content within information sources	Does the application have the capability to monitor content changes within information sources? (e.g., message pops up to inform about changes)
10. Monitoring of information sources	Does the application have the capability to monitor changes regarding information sources? (e.g., message pops up to inform about new addresses, address changes, addresses deleted)
11. Targeting of information within sources	Does the application have the capability to find specific pieces of information in particular sources? (e.g., running specific queries in preselected sources)
12. Filtering of information	Does the application have the capability to filter information to meet minimal CI needs? (e.g., highlighting search terms, summarizing articles)
13. Alerting of information	Does the application have the capability to notify users about new information? (e.g., push technology)

14. Importation of information	Does the application have the capability to import information in different formats? (e.g., HTML, PDF, Excel, Word, PowerPoint files)
15. Screening of information	Does the application have the capability to screen out redundant or repetitive information?
16. Rating of information	Does the application have a function for rating the qualitative value of information?

III. Organization, storage, and retrieval

17. Indexing	Does the application offer an indexing function?
18. Hierarchical linking	Does the application allow for hierarchical linking?
19. Cross-topic linking	Does the application allow for cross-topic linking?
20. Storage of variety of formats	Does the application store a variety of formats?
21. Storage capacity	Does the application store collected information as well as CI products?
22. Internal searching	Does the application offer an internal search facility?
23. Browsing	Does the application allow for browsing?

IV. Analysis of information

24. Variety of CI analytical techniques	Does the application offer a variety of CI analytical techniques? (e.g., three or more types of techniques, basic company profiles not considered here)
25. Level of analysis	Does the application allow for varying levels of analysis?
26. Synthesis of information	Does the application synthesize (summarize) information in any way?
27. Recommendations for action	Does the analysis result in recommendations for action?

V. Development of CI products

28. Variety of formats for viewing CI products	Does the application offer a variety of formats for viewing the final product?
29. Effectiveness of formats	Are the formats effective in conveying CI?
30. Flexibility for adapting CI products	Can one format be easily adapted to another format?

VI. Distribution of CI products	
31. Capacity for distributing CI products	Does the application offer a function for distributing intelligence?
32. Identification of potential CI consumers	Does the application help to identify potential CI consumers in the light of particular CI products?

for Competitive Intelligence Professionals (SCIP), Fuld & Co., and CI Resources Index, as well as through a Web search. The purpose was not to conduct an exhaustive search but to identify several off-the-shelf CI software packages that could be used to demonstrate our evaluation method. The software applications identified through this initial stage were carefully scrutinized and qualified on the basis of the following selection criteria:

- The software must perform at least three (preferably four or five) value-added processes similar to those outlined in the CI cycle.

- Those value-added processes must recognize the specific intelligence needs of the CI process.

- The software must perform some level of analysis.

Most of the software packages we looked at were excluded because they did not meet these minimum requirements; we were left with six products: Knowledge.Works, Market Signal Analyzer, Strategy!, Viva Intelligence Portal, Wincite, and Wisdom Builder. In each case, the software vendors were contacted to obtain free demonstration copies, and for permission to evaluate the software package and to publish the results. Of the six companies contacted, four responded favorably and made demonstration copies available through their Web sites: Knowledge.Works, Strategy!, Viva Intelligence Portal, and Wincite.

Evaluating software is not only a time-consuming and detailed operation, but it also involves some intuition. It is almost impossible to simulate a real scenario to evaluate software especially when access to the full application is not possible. Most demonstration copies of software applications are scaled-down versions of the full package and vary from unmanipulatable videos and PowerPoint presentations of the software, to offering time-limited full access to the entire software package. Evaluators must rely on the documentation that accompanies the software demonstration to fill in some of the gaps. Such documentation gives room to potential misinterpretation both in favor of and to the disadvantage of the product. Similarly, there are real time constraints placed on evaluators. Indeed, to really grasp the full capacity of a product, one could easily spend many weeks—even months—testing, examining, and deciphering a CI application. Unfortunately, neither evaluators nor potential technology users have that luxury. Thus, although evaluating software demonstration copies can provide a fairly good idea of the software, it rarely provides a complete picture.

On the other hand, evaluating software with full access is somewhat unrealistic. When the software is purchased, most require lengthy installation times and training programs for users (e.g., two full-time company representatives working for two weeks can be required), which cannot be accomplished when conducting an evaluation prior to purchase. Given the typical conditions under which most potential buyers evaluate software, it is impossible to gain insight into all of the capabilities of any application. It was under these conditions, with real-life conditions in mind, that our evaluation of the four software packages was conducted. This does not mean, of course, that a more thorough evaluation, involving more systematic testing, would not be appropriate. It is certainly the logical next step after the development of an evaluation model, as provided here.

Unlike other software evaluations, our goal was not to rank the applications, considering that the rapid pace of technology is likely to make such a ranking obsolete rather quickly. But, more importantly, our evaluation provides a comparative assessment of CI software applications from an information-processing perspective.

The basic evaluation was conducted using an evaluation table containing 32 evaluation questions (Table 5.2).

Software Evaluation

The software evaluation was conducted in 2002 using the most recent versions of the four software packages as well as the most recent documentation. A table summarizes the evaluation, or the answers to each evaluation question, and results are grouped according to the

Table 5.2   A Framework for Evaluating CI Software

Identification of CI Needs		Comments
1. Does the application help to identify the main CI client communities?	Yes No	
2. Does the application help to identify CI topics?	Yes No	
3. Does the application help to identify the pieces of information required to address the CI topics?	Yes No	
4. Does the application help to identify CI analytical techniques to address the needs of the CI clients?	Yes No	
5. Can the CI topics and analytical techniques be changed?	Yes No	

Acquisition of Competitive Information		Comments
6. Does the application help to identify external information sources?	Yes No	
7. Does the application help to identify internal information sources?	Yes No	
8. Does the application relate information sources with specific topics?	Yes No	
9. Does the application have the capability to monitor content changes within information sources?	Yes No	
10. Does the application have the capability to monitor changes regarding information sources?	Yes No	
11. Does the application have the capability to find specific pieces of information in particular sources?	Yes No	
12. Does the application have the capability to filter information to meet minimal CI needs?	Yes No	
13. Does the application have the capability to notify users about new information?	Yes No	
14. Does the application have the capability to import information in different formats?	Yes No	
15. Does the application have the capability to screen out redundant or repetitive information?	Yes No	
16. Does the application have a function for rating the qualitative value of information?	Yes No	

Organization, Storage, and Retrieval   Comments

17. Does the application offer an indexing function?	Yes No	
18. Does the application allow for hierarchical linking?	Yes No	
19. Does the application allow for cross-topic linking?	Yes No	
20. Does the application store a variety of formats?	Yes No	
21. Does the application store collected information as well as CI products?		
22. Does the application offer an internal search facility?	Yes No	
23. Does the application allow for browsing?	Yes No	

Analysis of Information   Comments

24. Does the application offer a variety of CI analytical techniques?	Yes No	
25. Does the application allow for varying levels of analysis?	Yes No	
26. Does the application synthesize (summarize) information in any way?	Yes No	
27. Does the analysis result in recommendations for action?	Yes No	

Development of CI Products   Comments

28. Does the application offer a variety of formats for viewing the final product?	Yes No	
29. Are the formats effective in conveying CI?	Yes No	
30. Can one format be easily adapted to another format?	Yes No	

Distribution of CI products   Comments

31. Does the application offer a function for distributing intelligence?	Yes No	
32. Does the application help to identify potential CI consumers in the light of particular CI products?	Yes No	

steps in the CI process. Each table is followed by a comparative description of each application and a discussion that highlights the main values added by each technology.

Identification of CI Needs

Table 5.3 summarizes the assessment of the products for the criteria related to the Identification of CI Needs step. Identifying the information needs is a critical aspect in determining the direction and focus of the CI process. For each of the five evaluation questions, the answers are provided on the basis of our understanding of the features of different software packages. Where it was unclear whether the product was able to meet our criteria, we put a question mark. Following the table, a detailed analysis for each product is provided.

Knowledge.Works

Knowledge.Works can be integrated within Lotus Notes or Microsoft Exchange/Outlook. The interfaces of these two platforms

Table 5.3   Identification of CI Needs

Identification of CI Needs—Summary				
Questions	Knowledge. Works	Strategy!	Viva Intelligence Portal	Wincite
1. Does the application help to identify the main CI client communities?	No	No	No	No
2. Does the application help to identify CI topics?	No	Yes	Yes	Yes
3. Does the application help to identify the pieces of information required to address CI topics?	No	Yes	Yes	Yes
4. Does the application help to identify CI analytical techniques to address the needs of the CI clients?	No	Yes	No	Yes
5. Can the CI topics and analytical techniques be changed?	Yes	?[1]	Yes	Yes

1. Question marks are used when it was unclear from the software demo whether the application is able to fulfill the criterion.

are slightly different, and we looked at both demos. Although the application was designed specifically for CI purposes, it offers no mechanism for identifying CI client communities. The "Key Intelligence Topics" (KITs) represent a central component of the software, but they are not specified, and it is up to the user to define what they should be. Basically, the application offers an empty field in which the administrator could add the intelligence topics. Consequently, Knowledge.Works does not identify the pieces of information needed to address the CI topics; however, as shown later in Table 5.5, it suggests some pieces of information to create company profiles. There are also no suggestions regarding categories of information that might be important to collect. A list of "Key Intelligence Questions" (KIQs) can be developed by the manager of the application, presumably in consultation with CI clients, to cover each topic, but they are not specified. This aspect of the software is unclear. These questions are probably worked out when the software is installed, and they might be customizable. It is clear that new questions can be saved within each topic. KITs and KIQs seem to be the backbone concepts behind the software, and they are linked to the "creation of intelligence" as opposed to the acquisition of intelligence.

Analytical tools are recommended in the form of "Competitor Matrices" and "Competitor Profiles," which seem to be, in fact, tools for visualizing and reporting information. "Competitor Matrices" offers a table for reporting some kind of data (not fully explained in the demo). For "Competitor Profiles," a number of headings such as Overview, History, News, Officers & Employees, Competitors, and Financials are provided. These headings are also used for storing content. Considering that the tool "Competitor Profiles" is a minimum to offer in such an application, and that it is more a fact sheet, Knowledge.Works does not offer a variety of analytical techniques. Intelligence Topics can be changed because they are not built in the application and can be adapted as needed.

Strategy!

Strategy! offers no mechanism to identify the intelligence consumer or facility to identify the intelligence needs of those consumers. Several important CI topics are identified:

- Goals

- Capabilities

- Strategy

- Assumptions

- Response profile for competitors

- Threat of substitution for substitute product providers

- Entry barriers for potential entrants

- Bargaining power for customers and suppliers

Strategy! does provide a lot of guidance to users as to the information needs required for the key intelligence topics. This is done in two ways. First, the help facility describes the Strategic Planning process and offers several examples of intelligence products. And, second, the detailed information needs are outlined by field names in the database. These include the broad topics of Companies, Products, and Industry. Each of these categories is then broken down into subcategories:

- Companies

- Our company

- Direct competitors

- Substitute product providers

- Potential entrants into the industry

- Customers

- Suppliers

One can drill down into these subcategories to uncover even more specific information requirements.

There are three main analytical techniques used by Strategy!: benchmarking, SWOT, and competitor response profile. For the most part, the users rather than the software conduct analysis, but the information requirements outlined by the software are related to the information requirements of these analytical techniques. It is unclear whether the field headings can be changed after the software has been implemented. However, the software does provide several unassigned fields that can be defined by the user.

Viva Intelligence Portal

The Viva Intelligence Portal offers no mechanism to identify the intelligence consumer or facility to identify the intelligence needs of those consumers. The CI topics outlined in this software are:

- Core competencies

- Objectives

- Strategy

- Strengths

- Weaknesses

- Opportunities

- Threats

The section entitled "BI-Elements" (as mentioned before, the software is designed by a Finnish company and, in Europe, BI for Business Intelligence is more or less the same as CI) presents four categories of information needs required to address the CI topics listed above:

- Companies

- Countries

- Industries

- Trends

Within these categories are subcategories of topics, for instance:

Companies

- Competitors

- Customers

- Suppliers

Countries

- Africa

- Asia-Pacific

- Middle East

- Europe

- North America

- Latin America

In some cases (e.g., Companies and Countries), the user can drill down into the subcategories to identify more specific information needs. Presumably, the topic "Countries," which lists continents, can be broken down into countries. The only analytical technique offered by Viva Intelligence Portal is benchmarking. "Company profiles" can be created, but they stand as basic fact sheets. In the "Tools" section of the software, the Viva Intelligence Portal offers an intelligence request form where intelligence consumers can provide their name, e-mail address, purpose of request, content requirements, output form, and deadline requirements. It was not clear, however, from the demo how the system administrator is alerted to this CI request. The field headings can be changed and adapted to the user's needs when the software is being implemented. It is not specified whether they can be changed and adapted after the software is in use.

Wincite

In the "Planning and Direction" section of the software is a field entitled "Targeted Company Users." In this space, the software users can specify who the main competitive intelligence consumer group is. Wincite does not offer a facility for querying intelligence consumers as to what their CI needs are. The software application identifies three broad categories of CI topics: companies, products, markets/regions. These categories are broken down into subcategories:

Companies

- Company Overview

- Company News

- Financial Information

- Acquisitions/Alliances

- Company SWOT

Products

- Product Overview

- Marketing Pricing

- Product SWOT

- Product Catalogs

Markets /Regions

- Market Overview

- Porter Market

- Supply Chain

The information requirements for each topic are broadly defined. The analytical techniques offered by Wincite are the following: Company and Product SWOT, Competitor Analysis, Sales Analysis, 4 Square Market Analysis, and the Porter Model. It is not clear from the demo version whether the CI topics can be changed, but it claims that some aspects of the software are customizable.

Discussion: Identification of CI Needs Capabilities

The four software packages approach the identification of needs process very differently, displaying a variety of strengths and weaknesses in this area. None of the four software packages offer any type of mechanism for identifying the intelligence consumer. The underlying assumption may be that a variety of management functions will require information/intelligence about competitors and competitive conditions. However, as discussed in Chapter 2, CI often requires a high level of analysis that is specifically tied to the intelligence needs of one consumer group. Thus, software that fails to identify, or facilitate the identification of, the main consumer groups is unlikely to perform a high level of analysis. Each package deals differently with CI topics as shown in Table 5.4.

As outlined in Table 5.4, only Knowledge.Works does not identify at least some key intelligence topics. Wincite offers three very basic and broad categories for topics. The subcategories of topics are in fact types of information that need to be collected or assembled. Topics identified by Strategy! are loosely based on the diagnostic components outlined by Porter in his model of Competitor Strategy, which includes: future goals, current strategy, assumptions, and capabilities,

Table 5.4 CI Topics Defined in Each Software Application

Knowledge.Works	**Strategy!**	**Viva Intelligence Portal**	**Wincite**
• Not pre-determined	• Goals • Capabilities • Strategy • Assumptions • Response Profile for competitors • Threat of substitution for substitute product providers • Entry barriers for Potential entrants • Bargaining power for customers and suppliers	• Core Competencies • Objectives • Strategy • Strengths • Weaknesses • Opportunities • Threats	• Companies • Products • Markets/Regions

combined with some other aspects (e.g., response profile for competitors, threat of substitution for substitute product providers, entry barriers for potential entrants, bargaining power for customers and suppliers). Interestingly, the meaning of these concepts has been adapted slightly. In Porter's theory, it is a company's future goals, current strategy, assumptions, and capabilities that determine a competitor's response profile. Thus, to reflect this in a software product, these concepts should be subcategories of the competitor's response profile, rather than each being individually considered as an intelligence topic, as is done in Strategy!.

The Viva Intelligence Portal identifies seven key intelligence topics that are loosely based on SWOT analytical techniques as well as Porter's framework for competitor analysis and bits and pieces from other approaches to CI.

All the applications try to direct the collection of information by identifying some types of information required, or CI information requirements, as shown in Table 5.5.

Strategy! fulfills the third criterion, "Does the application help to identify the pieces of information required to address the CI topics?" very well. Table 5.5 outlines the more general information requirements identified by Strategy! by way of field headings. For each of these general information requirements, the software also identifies in great detail the type of information required in each general category. For example, under the section "direct competitors," the user is required to include details about finances, operations, and so on. The other three software applications we tested outline only broad areas of information needed and do not provide the user with much guidance about detailed information requirements. For example, Knowledge.Works and Wincite both offer a section for competitors' financial information, but do not specify what types of financial information should be included here. Similarly, Knowledge.Works takes a somewhat loose approach in intermixing information requirements, such as "Location and Subsidiaries," "Products/ Operations," and "Competitors," with information sources and types of information, such as "Website" and "News and Commentary."

Both Strategy! and Wincite identify a number of CI analytical techniques while Knowledge.Works and Viva Intelligence Portal each identify only one (see Table 5.6). Although Wincite identifies several analytical techniques, it does not specify the detailed information requirements necessary for these techniques, which renders the

Table 5.5   CI Information Requirements Defined in Each Software Application

Knowledge.Works	Strategy!	Viva Intelligence Portal	Wincite
(for company profiles) Companies • Website • Overview • History • News & Commentary • Officers & Employees • Location & Subsidiaries • Products/ Operations • Competitors • Financials Reports	Companies • Our company • Direct competitors • Substitute product providers • Potential entrants into the industry • Customers • Suppliers Products • Our Products • Competitor Products Industry • Environment-Societal Expectations • Environment-Governmental Regulations • Market Share • Market Size • Exit Barriers • Innovation • Trends and Shifts	Companies • Competitors • Customers • Suppliers Countries • Africa • Asia-Pacific • Europe • Latin America • Middle East • North America Industries • To be identified by user Trends • To be identified by user	Companies • Company Overview • Company News • Financial Information • Acquisitions/ Alliances • Company SWOT Products • Product Overview • Marketing Pricing • Product SWOT • Product Catalogs Markets /Regions • Market Overview • Porter market • Supply Chain

Table 5.6   CI Analytical Techniques

Knowledge.Works	Strategy!	Viva Intelligence Portal	Wincite
• Competitor matrices	• Benchmarking • SWOT • Competitor response profile	• Benchmarking	• Product/company SWOT • Competitor analysis • Sales analysis • 4-Square market analysis • Porter model

analytical techniques almost useless. The strongest software application in this area is Strategy!, which identifies detailed CI topics, their corresponding information requirements, and the relevant analytical techniques necessary to transform information into intelligence. Viva Intelligence Portal is the only software package that offers a facility for the intelligence consumer to query the database with an intelligence request.

The CI topics can be customized for all software packages at the time that they are being implemented. However, with Strategy! it is unclear whether these topics can be changed after the application is up and running. The latest version of Wincite, with its "screen painter," is supposed to allow business analysts to add and modify the topic screens and fields, and seems to offer a high level of customization to the user. The KITs are not predefined in the Knowledge.Works application, so new KITs can be added at any time and old ones can be deleted. With Viva Intelligence Portal, the system administrator can change CI topics to meet the needs of the intelligence consumers, even after the software is in use.

Although Wincite has some very interesting features, Strategy! seems to be the strongest software for this step of the CI process because it provides a rich framework for intelligence topics and information requirements, and recommends several relevant analytical techniques. Viva Intelligence Portal and Wincite are less rich in these aspects. Viva Intelligence Portal provides a basic framework for both topics and information requirements, but only recommends one analytical technique. Wincite identifies relevant intelligence techniques but does not clearly outline the information requirements of these techniques. Knowledge.Works does not identify any key intelligence topics or information needs, leaving it to the user to define them, but may offer this consultation service during the installation process.

In terms of value-added processes, all applications do contribute to some extent to the value *selectivity* by requiring that users make choices at the input side of the system and by narrowing the content that should be integrated. However, the values *closeness to problem* and *precision* are not really addressed because specific user needs are not considered and the suggested topics remain very broad. The value *flexibility*, on the other hand, could not be assessed because the ways in which each application can be adapted remain unclear, or whether it could be done by the users.

Acquisition of Competitive Information

In Table 5.7, the software products are assessed according to the Acquisition of Competitive Information evaluation questions. This step in the CI cycle is extremely critical and goes beyond evaluating information sources or Web search capability. The value-added processes here should help to acquire information of quality that is relevant to the CI needs identified in the previous step.

Knowledge.Works

Regarding the first evaluation question, identification of information sources, Knowledge.Works identifies two types of relevant sources: "Human Documents" and "Written Documents." This classification is very similar to the conceptual view of CI as developed by Fuld & Co. (2002), which proposes "primary sources" (or Human Documents) and "published information" (or Written Documents). The Human Documents section offers interfaces to collect Field Contributions, Conference Contributions, Interviews, and Contacts. A discussion forum is offered, indicating the need for collecting information from those in the field, in the form of a message board. To collect information from people, four types of CI communities can be created: restricted and moderated, restricted and unmoderated, unrestricted and moderated, unrestricted and unmoderated. Such community creation is intended to allow the members of each community to contribute content. Unfortunately, the exact meaning of these types of communities is not clearly explained in the demo.

In the "Written Documents" section, several types of written documents are specified with Lotus Notes (News Articles, Web Sites, Market Research, Company Profiles, Company Matrix, Office Documents, Daily Briefs, and Flash Reports) and with Microsoft Exchange/Outlook (News Articles, Web News, Web Sites, Specialty Reports, Research Reports, Research Tools, Reports, and News Flashes). It is worth mentioning that the demo creates some confusion about the nature of these documents. For instance, "Research Tools" are associated with a search engine such as AltaVista and an information source such as the BBC Web site. A search engine is not a document and an information source does not help to find information on the Web: They have two different functions, and it is somewhat odd to see them in the same category. The software

Table 5.7   Acquisition of Information

Acquisition of Information – Summary				
Questions	1	2	3	4
6. Does the application help to identify external information sources?	No	No	No	Yes
7. Does the application help to identify internal information sources?	No	No	No	No
8. Does the application relate information sources with specific topics?	No	No	No	Yes
9. Does the application have the capability to monitor content changes within information sources?	Yes	No	No	No
10. Does the application have the capability to monitor changes regarding information sources?	No	No	No	No
11. Does the application have the capability to find specific pieces of information in particular sources?	Yes	No	No	Yes
12. Does the application have the capability to filter information to meet minimal CI needs?	Yes	No	No	No
13. Does the application have the capability to notify users about new information?	Yes	No	Yes	No
14. Does the application have the capability to import information in different formats?	No	Yes	Yes	Yes
15. Does the application have the capability to screen out redundant or repetitive information?	No	No (Yes with other tool)	No	No
16. Does the application have a function for rating of the qualitative value of information?	Yes	Yes	Yes (for sources)	No

1: Knowledge.Works
2: Strategy!
3: Viva Intelligence Portal
4: Wincite

does not recommend specific external sources of information (such as LexisNexis or Dialog). For internal sources, having "Office Documents" in the list is not really useful because there are no pointers to specific internal documents that should be consulted. In fact, sources for collecting information are mixed with types of CI products that could be produced such as Daily Briefs and Flash Reports. Moreover, the application does not relate information sources to specific topics.

The application offers a facility for monitoring content changes within information sources by regularly searching in specific sources. However, changes about sources (whether a new source is created or another one is deleted) are not monitored. Using Web crawlers to scan the Internet, it does retrieve content from predesignated sources, and news can be input automatically or manually. The interface can be adapted so that the news (titles and summaries) can scroll down on one side of the interface. It is possible to filter the information by limiting the number of hits by subject, competitor, region, and source. Filtering is achieved also by a Text Summarizer, which basically limits the length of an article by showing only its title and the first few lines of text. The system administrator determines the length of the text summary. This summarization does not involve any semantic searching or manipulation. The application does not offer a facility to screen out redundant information, or documents with similar content.

For acquiring information, two search engines are available on the interface: internal (for searching in folders) and external (for searching on the Internet). With the Lotus platform, advanced search and search profiles capabilities are included. Although, there is an internal search facility, it does not seem to allow searches in internal documents or databases; rather this is determined by the information architecture of the organization.

Interestingly, before written documents are stored, it is possible to rate their content (e.g., routine, critical, interesting, poor quality, potential evidence). When content comes from "human documents," it is possible to rate the human source reliability (e.g., probably reliable, questionable, unknown, very reliable). The application does not offer a facility for importing information in different formats, and it seems designed primarily to handle text documents. Importation of new information can be done but it is not automatic. For example, users can be notified automatically of news titles, so alerting is possible based on their search profiles, but the system administrator must save the content manually.

Strategy!

Strategy! does not help to identify relevant information sources and there is no Web crawler embedded in the application. It is, however, possible to create a list of information sources, providing links to those that are electronic and references to paper-based sources. Users can find information about sources (usually by name of publication or person) such as brief description, date of origin, date recorded, format, physical location information, Web location information, unique number, and contact name. This allows users to easily return to the original source for reference purposes or to go back to the source for updates.

The application does not relate information sources to specific topics. It does not offer a facility for monitoring content changes within information sources nor for monitoring information sources. Users can search for information on the Web using search engines already available. The application does not offer alert facilities, and there is no mechanism (such as a text summarizer or matching search profiles) for filtering information. However, a companion tool, *In Touch*, screens out entries to avoid duplication. This is a major strength. Another strength is the ability to import Excel spreadsheets into the database.

Information can be added to the database in two ways: predefined fields can be filled in either using the keyboard or by copy/cut and paste. The application offers a functionality for rating the credibility of an information source when content is added to the *Scratch Pad*. This feature is used by people in the field who want to add content to the database.

Viva Intelligence Portal

Viva Intelligence Portal does not help to identify relevant information sources. An information source directory can be created and can be searched in the "Info Sources" section. The idea is, as with Strategy!, to store contact information about sources according to the type of information that they contain. For example, under "Competitor Research," users can list competitor Web sites, relevant news sources, and/or internal employees who may have information about a competitor. The sources are listed and described. A usage guide, an analysis of the source, and a link to the sources can be provided.

The application does not offer a facility for monitoring content changes within information sources nor for monitoring information sources. It has no embedded Web crawler, although it is possible to search for specific pieces of information using standard Web search engines as the application is entirely Web-based (Microsoft Internet Explorer). There is no mechanism for filtering information. The application does, however, offer a particular type of alert facility referred to as a "Personal Intelligence Service." Individual consumers can create a Personal Intelligence Profile by choosing a subject from a list of descriptors: companies (competitors, customers, or suppliers), countries, industries, and trends. The software will automatically alert the user when a new piece of information is added to the system. A new document, for example, will be tagged with the same descriptor used for defining the Personal Intelligence Profile. The alert will then notify the user that a new document is available. Note that this type of alert does not advise the user of new information posted on the Web.

The application seems to offer a facility for importing information in different formats such as PDF, HTML, and MS Word. However, the importation of spreadsheets does not seem possible. Information is acquired either through cut and paste function or by entering it manually with the keyboard. The application offers a facility for assigning a value judgment to information sources, rather than the actual information acquired. The sources are evaluated according to how they match information needs of CI, their format and availability, and the level of analysis and forecasts they provide.

Wincite

Wincite identifies several relevant information sources for CI that are available for free on the Web. For example, the topic (and screen) "Financial Summary" directs users to a number of sources (Morningstar, CBS Marketwatch, First Call, etc.), and the "News Summary" provides links to company Web sites, newspapers, business magazines, trade papers, and search engines. Therefore, it helps identify sources and relates some sources to certain topics. Regarding internal sources, the demo does not suggest typical sources but rather broad types of documents (Excel, PowerPoint, charts, etc.). The strength of the application is in maintaining hyperlinks to all these external and internal sources. The application does not offer a facility for monitoring content changes within information sources nor changes regarding information sources. However, for targeting information, searches can be launched on many topic screens at any time using subjects, ticker codes, and even field values, such as the date. Some form of push technology is integrated, similar to that employed by Viva Intelligence Portal, in order to send alert reports to CI clients. Therefore, users are notified about new CI products that are created (from a distribution point of view) but not when new information is acquired. No facility is available to import information in different formats because the application is not a database but is used with databases such as Oracle, Microsoft Access, and SQL Server. However, it can display Excel charts and tables. As with most of the CI applications we evaluated, there is no facility to screen out redundant information, and there is no means for rating the value of information.

Discussion: Acquisition of Competitive Information Capabilities

The software applications we studied differ in their methods for acquiring information. Knowledge.Works features an original categorization of human and written documents that recognizes the importance of human beings as CI information sources. However, only Wincite offers specific pointers to external information sources available on the Web. Only Knowledge.Works helps the user monitor content changes in information sources by querying information in specific sources automatically on a regular basis. Both Knowledge.Works and Wincite allow the targeting of information sources because direct links to sources are maintained on the screen. With all four applications, the information must be input manually because none offers a mechanism for automatic importation.

All four evaluated applications, however, allow the creation of information source directories. Viva Intelligence Portal is particularly strong in this area, offering a facility for identifying, describing, locating, and assessing information sources. The sources are categorized according to what type of information can be acquired from them, ultimately reducing time for discovering and acquiring information. Knowledge.Works and Viva Intelligence Portal permit the sharing of information, allowing human sources to add data in a discussion forum in the former and as "hot signals" in the latter.

Surprisingly, facilities for monitoring the relevance of content and information sources as time passes are weak: None of the programs offer sophisticated information tracking capabilities for monitoring changes within information sources and for monitoring sources. Monitoring changes within sources involves tracking the changes in the content of a Web site or a database while monitoring sources consists of tracking changes to the actual sources. For example, new information sources may appear, electronic Web addresses and titles may change, or other sources may disappear or no longer be relevant.

Neither Strategy! nor Viva Intelligence Portal has incorporated capabilities for finding (or targeting) specific information. Wincite is interoperable with Internet Explorer or Netscape Navigator, and Knowledge.Works has incorporated Web-searching capabilities into the software. The fact that CI information should come from a variety of sources is not reflected in these packages: All focus on collecting information via the Web—just one potential source. These applications could be greatly improved by incorporating a facility for finding information on the company intranet, as well. All the packages allow only basic cut-and-paste and keyboard entry facilities for inputting information. Strategy! offers an extra feature for importing Excel spreadsheets, which is mainly useful for inputting financial information for benchmarking of competitors. Wincite allows the consultation of files other than text documents and Viva Intelligence Portal can handle various formats but not spreadsheets.

Another weakness of these applications is the lack of mechanisms for filtering information. Knowledge.Works is the only application that offers a type of filtering through its "summarizing documents" feature. All of these programs would be significantly improved if sophisticated filtering technologies were incorporated.

Closely related to filtering technologies are alerting technologies. Two of the software packages we looked at—Knowledge.Works and Viva Intelligence Portal—include an alerting function. Both employ push technology to deliver information to the desktop based on a predefined profile, thus ignoring information that the profile indicates is not relevant. None of the applications incorporates any type of technology to screen out redundant information. Only Strategy! offers a companion tool for such a process. The incorporation of a feature that would screen out redundant information would significantly improve these applications, considering that all of the software packages rely heavily on the Web as an important source of information. As anyone who has searched the Web knows, the amount of redundancy in the information available there is huge (e.g., many news articles reporting the same thing).

We did find some mechanisms for rating the quality, reliability, or credibility of the information and/or information sources in the applications. On the whole, these mechanisms are very basic, and only Viva Intelligence Portal offers a facility for assigning a value to the information source rather than to the actual information acquired. KnowledgeWorks and Strategy! allow users to rate the information content. Ideally, applications should offer both options. Evaluating the quality of the source (for instance a rumor as opposed to a newspaper article) is as important as assessing the quality of the information provided by the source because it contributes to the evaluation of the content and guides information acquisition strategy. Although current technology does not allow software to evaluate the reliability of information sources without human interaction, we believe CI software manufacturers would add value to their products if they offered a facility whereby the user can indicate the reliability of sources as information and links to information sources are added.

In general, all four software packages rate quite poorly when it comes to acquiring information. The main value that could be added by technology is *linkage*, by providing pointers to existing resources to expand acquisition strategies, and *precision*, by avoiding too much noise in the system. The fact that some push technologies are offered yet are not combined with mechanisms to ensure the elimination of redundant information suggests that *noise reduction* has not been thoroughly addressed.

Organization, Storage, and Retrieval

Our assessment of the software packages' abilities to perform the organization, storage, and retrieval process is presented in Table 5.8. The applications were generally successful in meeting our evaluation criteria for this step of the CI cycle.

Knowledge.Works

Knowledge.Works involves the use of keywords to categorize, retrieve, and view content of articles (by competitor, date last modified, date created, article date, source, industry, region, author title, and URL). Other documents can be stored by subject, competitor,

Table 5.8   Organization, Storage, and Retrieval

Organization, Storage and Retrieval – Summary				
Questions	1	2	3	4
17. Does the application offer an indexing function?	Yes	Yes	Yes	Yes
18. Does the application allow for hierarchical linking?	No	Yes	No	Yes
19. Does the application allow for cross-topic linking?	Yes	Yes	Yes	Yes
20. Does the application store a variety of formats?	?	Yes	Yes	No
21. Does the application store collected information as well as CI products?	Yes	Yes	Yes	No
22. Does the application offer an internal search facility?	Yes	Yes	Yes	Yes
23. Is the browsing function effective?	?	Yes	?	No

1: Knowledge.Works
2: Strategy!
3: Viva Intelligence Portal
4: Wincite

region, product, sources, and other criteria. There is not, however, a controlled vocabulary. Indexing is possible, but its quality is directly related to administrators' competencies and consistency. Documents can be stored in folders on an internal database in Lotus Notes or on a public directory with Microsoft Outlook/Exchange. Because the application does not come with a thesaurus or controlled vocabulary, there is no hierarchical linking between documents; neither categories nor keywords are organized in subcategories. Cross-topic linking is possible because documents can be filed under various keywords (for example, a subject, a competitor name, a product name, and a region). The key question here is whether, in the absence of a controlled vocabulary, the organization of files can be efficiently maintained. Different types of documents can be stored: news items, news articles, Web sites, specialty publications, research reports, research tools, daily briefs, competitor matrices, and competitor profiles, to name some. Web sites can be stored as live links or as stored pages. Therefore, the collected information and resultant CI products can be placed easily into word processing documents. It is unclear, however, whether the application can handle numerical documents such as spreadsheets, or presentation documents (e.g., PowerPoint files), which is why the criterion on the storage of a variety of formats raised a question mark.

As already mentioned, an internal search facility is available (Quick Search and Advanced Search). The inclusion of a "browsing" feature implies that one may browse the Knowledge.Works folders without searching for specific content. It is possible to browse individual folders, but it is unclear from the demo whether the content of all the folders that are managed within the system can be viewed on the screen at one time, or can be listed for easy perusal.

Strategy!

Strategy! is designed as a relational database tool and requires that information content be indexed with field names and stored accordingly. A basic internal search facility allows the location of information in the database. Users can search by company, product, or person. A list of companies, products, or people then pops up which users can browse. Hierarchical and cross-topic links between documents are facilitated. For example, in the category "competitor," various competitors are listed and, for each, products are listed and linked to similar products offered by the user's company and other competitors. The indexing function is quite comprehensive. As previously mentioned, the application can store a variety of formats and both the collected information and the CI products can be stored. From the demo, Strategy! is the only package that clearly allows browsing in the database; it is possible to see the whole structure and the various links between documents. Thus, someone who does not know what to search for can scan the database easily.

Viva Intelligence Portal

Viva Intelligence Portal is called a "portal" because it is a Web-based technology; however, it operates within an intranet or as a hosted service. Content can be stored as CI Products (news, hot signals from within the organization, company and country profiles, and research and analysis documents) and organized according to CI elements (Company intelligence, Country intelligence, and Industry intelligence). This structure allows users to retrieve, for example, News grouped into Companies, Countries, and Industries, with information on Competitors grouped in CI products such as news, hot signals, and research and analyses. There is no hierarchical linking because CI elements do not have many subcategories, but cross-topic linking is possible. No controlled vocabulary is provided to select appropriate keywords. The application supports all MS Office and PDF documents. An internal search functionality is available and information can be sorted by date and relevance. It is unclear from the demo whether the database can be browsed.

Wincite

Wincite is presented as a relational database, but in fact it requires pre-existing database platforms (such as Microsoft SQL or Oracle); thus, its capacity for organization, storage, and retrieval of information depends on these platforms. An indexing function is provided, but it is impossible to see with the demo how it works. We assume that hierarchical and cross-topic links can be established between documents given the typical capacity of the required platforms and because CI topics can be linked to subjects and fields. As the documentation shows, content can be assigned topics, subjects, and field values (year). However, there is no controlled vocabulary. Instead of storing documents, the application saves links to documents or hyperlinks. For example, the demo indicates that links to spreadsheets, presentations, charts, maps, Web sites, and news services can be saved. Therefore, it appears that the storage of a variety of formats and of information and CI products is not possible, although links are stored. An internal search facility is offered. Given that the application represents an interface to view information rather than an information system per se, it is evident that browsing is not possible. To find information, one must use the search facility with precise search criteria. The latest version includes additional features for displaying search results. When a search is launched, Wincite provides a list of hits ordered according to the degree by which they match the search terms, along with a brief summary of each selected document.

Discussion: Organization, Storage, and Retrieval Capabilities

The effective organization, storage, and retrieval of information collected for CI ensures that control over that information is maintained to guarantee its availability and, thus, its usefulness to the organization. Strategy! appears to be the most sophisticated application in this area in that it incorporates all the features of a database management system. The other three products we evaluated demonstrated only very basic indexing function and search facility. Similarly, the hierarchical and cross-topic links in those programs are limited to a number of topics—mainly companies, competitors, and products (linked to company names). This limitation might create some problems with topics like "regulations" or "government funding" because they cannot be indexed under companies, competitors, or products as they relate to the industry as a whole. Our evaluation, however, is limited by the fact that none of the demos other than that for Strategy! clearly showed or explained the mechanisms by which information is organized and retrieved. This dimension is indeed more "behind the scenes," and demos are typically oriented to show only what is "on the scene." Manufacturers place an emphasis on providing an adaptable interface that fulfills the needs of CI analysts, rather than providing a detailed explanation of the basic structure of their application.

In terms of Taylor's (1986) framework, specifically the mechanisms ensuring the values of *intellectual access*, *ordering*, and *precision*, only the Strategy! demo addresses these values outright. However, it is impossible to test in any way, with demos, the extent to which they are addressed. There is, in addition, a certain concern for flexibility and physical accessibility for storing different formats and information as well as CI products. Only Strategy! and Viva Portal Intelligence provide systems that clearly handle various formats and outcomes.

Analysis of Information

Table 5.9 shows our assessment of software packages according to their ability to perform the Analysis of Information step. The evaluation questions presented for this step are only four in number; however, the ability of software to perform this step is key to its ability to perform CI. As you can see, this step represents a major challenge for the CI software packages evaluated here.

Knowledge.Works

The only analytical tool that Knowledge.Works provides is its "Competitor Matrix," which is a table that allows for some comparisons. In the past, the real strength of this application was its interoperability with IBM's Intelligent Miner for Text (Fuld & Co., 2002),

Table 5.9   Analysis of Information

Analysis of Information – Summary				
Questions	1	2	3	4
24. Does the application offer a variety of CI analytical techniques?	No	Yes	No	Yes
25. Does the application allow for varying levels of analysis?	No	Yes	No	Yes
26. Does the application synthesize (summarize) information in any way?	No	No	No	No
27. Does the analysis result in recommendations for action?	No	No	No	No

1: Knowledge.Works
2: Strategy!
3: Viva Intelligence Portal
4: Wincite

which is used for analyzing the content of text documents by searching for specific terms (e.g., name of people, dates, places) or for key concepts, among other things. However, this option is no longer mentioned in the promotional materials (as of October, 2002). It may be that the integration of this tool with Knowledge.Works is no longer possible, or simply that it is no longer advertised. If the former is the case, the capability of Knowledge.Works will be greatly diminished.

Strategy!

Strategy! provides for three types of analysis (benchmarking, SWOT, and competitor response profile) that contribute to the comparison and categorization of data and information. Although the real analysis is done by the user of the application, Strategy! is quite sophisticated in offering various attributes to be selected by the user in order to create reports. For example, to create a company report, the user must choose among seven categories of organizations: our company, competitors, potential entrants, substitute producers, suppliers, customers, or senators.

Depending on the types of company reports that need to be created, the topic "Strategy" could be covered and one must select among the following attributes: company background, administration, finance, human resources, marketing operations, research and development, sales, service, target customer group, value leadership, and interrelation of functional areas. For another topic, "Entry Barriers," the following attributes are available: company background, access to distribution channels, capital requirements, differentiation and loyalty, economies of scale, government policy, government subsidy, learning and experience curve, location, pricing and margins, proprietary technology, switching costs, and access to raw materials.

All these attributes constitute a rich framework for enhancing analysis because they provide interesting pointers for gathering and examining information. To create product reports, product attributes are extremely well developed—their selection will determine varying ways of comparing information—and encompass the following items: market share, strengths and weaknesses, strategic strengths, differentiation, how to sell against, specifications, information resources, ad frequency by media type, availability by region, calling plan limitations, complaint rate, customer service ratings, customizations to base product, distribution, expenditures to promote this product, fine print details, insurance coverage requirements, languages available, lead time by region, manufacturing indicators, number of products shipped by region, product options, production plants, promotions and incentives, return statistics, services options, service plan details, warranty details, and win/loss sales statistics. There is no doubt that this extensive listing of items can help make users aware of the various types of data that may be analyzed for competitive purposes. Another strong feature of Strategy! is the ability to generate various charts and graphs, including quantitative and qualitative information representations.

Viva Intelligence Portal

Viva Intelligence Portal provides only one analytical tool: "benchmarking." This tool involves identifying for a given company a number of items: core competencies, objectives, strategy, strengths, weaknesses, opportunities, and threats. After the information under each item is filled in, the user can click on a button "benchmark" to generate a comparative table. Therefore, the analytical technique is rather a tool for creating a CI product.

Wincite

Wincite is the package that offers the largest number of analytical techniques (SWOT, Competitor Analysis, Sales Analysis, 4 Square

Market Analysis, and Porter Model). However, none of these analytical tools are automated: The application offers analytical frameworks or screens with empty boxes that must be filled in by a CI specialist. For example, for a SWOT analysis, it is possible to make a table listing the strengths, weaknesses, opportunities, and threats for several companies for comparison purposes. The Porter Model involves five empty fields (new entries, competitors, markets served, suppliers, and substitutions), but no explanations on how to fill them. It may be possible to generate some charts and graphs (for "Sales Analysis"), but how they are generated is unclear. Because many techniques are available and are complementary, it appears that various levels of analysis can be reached using Wincite. There is no attempt however, to help the formulation of recommendations for action.

Discussion: Analysis of Information Capabilities

As shown in Table 5.6, three of the four packages evaluated offer some CI analytical techniques. Viva Intelligence Portal and Knowledge.Works offer only two basic techniques. Strategy and Wincite are superior in allowing the manipulation of information and, thus, in letting users execute various types of analysis. Although Knowledge.Works integrates a Text Summarizer, this does not increase the level of analysis significantly, although it does allow scanning of the information. A good analysis is not complete if it is not accompanied by recommendations regarding future decisions or actions. This is considered the highest level of analysis possible, because it means weighing a number of organizational factors in relation to the outcomes reached through the analysis of competitors. Not surprisingly, none of these packages facilitate the development of recommendations for action.

Indeed, we were not surprised to discover that the analytical dimension of CI is not very well addressed by any of the packages, as analysis requires a significant application of human intelligence. However, given the fact that analysis is the crucial step to transforming information into intelligence, it is disappointing to see that the help function provided by these packages is so limited. In most cases, empty fields in the form of boxes are presented to the user, who has to figure out what to input. What values, then, are added by these software packages in the analysis step of the CI cycle? We could argue that these applications structure competitive information to facilitate its analysis. However, word processing and/or spreadsheet applications also allow the creation of templates that could fulfill this function (although less attractively, perhaps). Strategy! demonstrates the greatest value here for the pointers it provides to CI analysts, even though the largest range of analytical tools is offered by Wincite.

Development of CI Products

Table 5.10 presents our assessment of the software packages' ability to develop various CI products. The software packages performed well in the first two evaluation areas, but three of four received a question mark in the area of adaptability.

Knowledge.Works

It is possible to create a number of report types with Knowledge.Works (for example, "Daily Briefs," "News Flashes," and "Matrices"). After the acquisition of content (e.g., an article), a Daily Brief report can be created showing three major headings: Summary, Implications, and Details. Documents can be saved as Microsoft Word or Knowledge.Works documents. The examples available in the demo are not very attractive. The headings of the Daily Brief report are not very meaningful (e.g., Summary, Implications, and Details) and can be more of a hindrance than an asset because, in the course of the CI activities, it might be too early to summarize the implications of a report.

Table 5.10   Development of CI Products

Development of CI Products—Summary				
Questions	1	2	3	4
28. Does the application offer a variety of formats for viewing the final product?	Yes	Yes	Yes	Yes
29. Are the formats effective in conveying CI?	No	Yes	Yes	Yes
30. Can one format be easily adapted to another format?	?	Yes	?	?

1: Knowledge.Works
2: Strategy!
3: Viva Intelligence Portal
4: Wincite

Strategy!

Final products in Strategy! take the form of Company reports and Product reports. The application offers more than 150 templates for reporting information (e.g., Relative Strengths and Weaknesses of Two Products in text and graphic versions, Product or Service Comparison Matrix, Competitor Activity by Market Segments, and Product or Service List by Category). The scope of the information included in a report is almost entirely up to the user. Reports can be saved in a number of different formats: HTML, RTF, MSWord, Excel, Exchange folder, PDF, and Lotus Notes compatible files. Formats can be easily adapted.

Viva Intelligence Portal

The main presentation format offered by Viva Intelligence Portal is the company profile. This can be viewed as a single company profile or several companies can be benchmarked against one another. Profiles combine both text and a variety of graphs and figures for financial information. The user can choose the subjects to be included in the profile from a list of items (for example, General Information, Key Figures, Operations, and Technology). The report formats are effective for conveying CI because they include conceptualizing numerical data as well as text documents. The company profile format is not changeable or adaptable; it can be expanded to include additional subjects or reduced to include fewer subjects. The figures/graphs can be changed in a manner similar to that of MS Word.

Wincite

Wincite has two main report formats: The "Browser Profile Report," which contains text only, about a single company, and the "Browser Benchmark Report," which contains text about two or more companies benchmarked according to chosen characteristics. A CI Newsletter template is also provided as a screen for capturing information, and this is transformed as a profile report format. It seems that the software can perform some level of information visualization because it has set functions such as charts and diagrams; however, we were unable to test this in the demo provided to us for the evaluation. Text, graph, and diagram formats are all effective in conveying CI. The ability of the software to adapt from one format to another could not be demonstrated using the demo.

Discussion: Development of CI Products Capabilities

The software applications were quite varied in their ability to perform the "Presentation of CI Products" step. Strategy! is the strongest here, offering many formats for viewing CI and allowing users to choose which variables to include in the final product. Viva Intelligence Portal and Wincite offered some flexibility in presenting the intelligence product, but offered less flexibility than Strategy!. Knowledge.Works offers very little to the user in the way of presentation formats. The greatest value that a software package could add in the development of CI products is formatting, and this is certainly achieved by all the applications. However, the effectiveness of the formats regarding the values *simplicity* and *validity* is puzzling. On one hand, an application like Knowledge.Works offers formats that are very simple; on the other hand, Strategy!, Viva Intelligence Portal, Wincite, offer formats in their demo that seem complicated to use and may be restrictive for the users (e.g., the obligation to put information in a given field or under a given heading). Designing nice reports is not the main objective here. The format should be chosen based on how well it conveys the meaning of information and its analysis. Nonetheless, we conclude that Strategy!, Viva Intelligence Portal, and Wincite offer somewhat effective formats. The value *flexibility* is not obviously addressed in the demos because the extent to which a format can be easily transformed into another is not clearly demonstrated by any of the packages.

Distribution of CI Products

Table 5.11 presents our assessment of the software packages' ability to perform the Distribution of CI Products step in the CI Process. This assessment contains two evaluation questions, one of which was well fulfilled by all of the software packages and one of which was poorly fulfilled.

All the software applications we evaluated offer some mechanisms for distributing CI products. As for the acquisition of information, Knowledge.Works allows the creation of online communities of CI clients (restricted and moderated, restricted and unmoderated, unrestricted and moderated, unrestricted and unmoderated). From the demonstration copy, it is impossible to know the exact meaning of these terms, but clearly the idea is to allow different types of access to

Table 5.11   Distribution of CI Products

Distribution of CI Products—Summary				
Questions	1	2	3	4
31. Does the application offer a function for distributing intelligence?	Yes	Yes	Yes	Yes
32. Does the application help to identify potential CI consumers in the light of particular CI products?	No	No	No	No

1: Knowledge.Works
2: Strategy!
3: Viva Intelligence Portal
4: Wincite

the application. In addition, Knowledge.Works reports can be e-mailed to CI clients on a regular basis. With Strategy!, reports can be sent easily by e-mail. This option is also possible with Viva Intelligence Portal which, as previously mentioned, allows personal alerts. Wincite integrates an e-mail capability as well as an option for sending daily news alerts to CI clients. The need for rapid distribution and for physical accessibility to CI products is well addressed by all applications. However, none of them has a feature for identifying, once the CI products are designed, additional CI clients that were not identified at the outset. As these potential clients are not, presumably, on a distribution list, it is left up to the CI analysts to provide them with reports.

Global Assessment

The complete results of the assessment of all four packages are presented in Table 5.12. For each step, the number of yes and no responses to the evaluation questions are provided, along with the question marks for those questions we were not able to answer from the demos. The last row is a sum of these responses, and provides an interesting indication of the strengths and weaknesses of the CI software applications evaluated.

It is apparent that the various applications have different strengths and weaknesses. For instance, Knowledge.Works is strong

Table 5.12 Summary of Evaluation

STEPS	Knowledge.Works	Strategy!	Viva Intelligence Portal	Wincite
Identification of CI Needs	1 Yes 4 No	3 Yes 1 No 1 ?	3 Yes 2 No	4 Yes 1 No
Acquisition of Competitive Information	5 Yes 6 No	2 Yes 9 No	3 Yes 8 No	4 Yes 7 No
Organization, Storage, and Retrieval	4 Yes 1 No 2 ?	7 Yes	5 Yes 1 No 1 ?	4 Yes 3 No
Analysis of Information	4 No	2 Yes 2 No	4 No	2 Yes 2 No
Development of CI Products	1 No 1 Yes 1 ?	3 Yes	2 Yes 1 ?	2 Yes 1 ?
Distribution of CI Products	1 Yes 1 No	1 Yes 1 No	1 Yes 1 No	1 Yes 1 No
TOTAL	12 Yes 17 No 3 ?	18 Yes 13 No 1 ?	14 Yes 16 No 2 ?	17 Yes 14 No 1 ?

for acquiring information. Strategy! is interesting for the organization, storage, and retrieval of information and for the development of CI products. Wincite does not have a particular strength but meets many criteria, as does Viva Intelligence Portal. In terms of values, our evaluation shows that these CI software packages add only about 50 percent of the potential values—the number of "yes" answers to evaluation questions range between 12 and 18 out of 32—that information systems could bring to CI. It is interesting to see the extent to which various CI concepts and techniques are integrated. Unfortunately, these software applications are far from being "intelligent systems" because the role of human agents as system administrators, CI analysts, and information specialists is clearly essential to ensuring that they are used effectively.

Our evaluation further reveals that software vendors do not all release the same amount of information about their products. From the demos, it was impossible to examine and test some dimensions of the programs. Many claims found in the publicity are enticing, but the verification of their validity was simply not feasible. Given that all these packages require some level of customization before they can be put to practical use, a potential buyer must be convinced of the value of these products to contact these vendors because there is not always sufficient grounds for acknowledging such a value. On the other hand, one can argue that anything that supports the CI process in an organization is worthwhile, and, in that respect, all four packages offer some value.

Competitive Intelligence Technology—Summary, Implications, and Trends

The importance of developing CI strategies in various business sectors has been recognized for many years now, including, most recently, in the service sector (Sawyer, 2002). Increased globalization and market volatility create difficult conditions for companies. If they do not monitor their competitors, they are in danger of being outmaneuvered by them. The risks of ignoring competitors are great and include missed strategic opportunities, loss of significant market share, and even bankruptcy. The "competitive imperative," more global than ever (Gordon, 2002), influences all aspects of corporate decision making. Indeed, the days of stable business environments, when "large and even small companies knew exactly their market place" (Dou et al., 1993, p. 35), are well behind us. As with other business functions, companies are turning to technology to increase their ability to perform CI. In fact, it is nearly impossible in today's business environment to conduct CI without the use of computing technology at some level. The proliferation of information and information sources renders the tasks of watching, collecting, and analyzing information extremely daunting. And, certainly the value of CI has increased tremendously with the advent of new technologies. Never before have businesses had access to such a rich amount of information. While CI once suffered from a paucity of useful information, it must now struggle with information overload.

Although CI has gained widespread acceptance as a business function, a lack of consensus persists about the role of new technology in the CI process. The market for CI software is broad, thus confusing CI practitioners and software consumers. The interpretation of "CI software" can range from Web search engines to database platforms and to more sophisticated, full-blown CI applications. However, upon close examination we find that the majority of the products marketed as CI software facilitate one or more specific activities, such as acquiring information, rather than the entire CI process. While these packages can be very useful in conducting CI, they are not CI software per se.

In this book, the CI process has been deconstructed into its individual steps in order to identify the specific tasks that add value to information and the particular areas in which technology can help. We have presented a conceptual framework and a methodology for comparing and assessing software products available to help with CI-related activities, and, thus, for understanding the potential of these products to add value to information. This detailed conceptualization of the CI process can also be used to examine a CI function that is performed by analysts rather than by a software application. Companies can map the specific tasks being performed in their CI departments with the detailed CI process outlined here to identify gaps and improve CI functioning.

Chapter 1 raised a number of issues associated with the notions of value and information. Although information is a resource, it has some unique characteristics. Information has a primarily extrinsic value, and this value is almost completely subjective. Information may be valuable in one context, but not in another. Similarly, information that may be valuable to one individual, given his or her knowledge base, may be of no value to another. Thus, the value of information is directly tied to the purpose of the task at hand and an existing knowledge base. The value of any particular piece of information for CI will vary greatly because the purpose of CI is continually changing. Additionally, the value of CI information is directly related to the context in which it exists and depends a great deal on whether the use of intelligence is valued in the organization, and whether informed decision making is the result.

Similarly, value can be added to information in a number of ways. Because CI adds value through transforming information into intelligence, the distinctions between the concepts of knowledge, intelligence, information, and data provide insight into the process of CI. Even though the definitions of these concepts involve many overlaps, information is generally thought to become intelligence through the activities of acquiring, organizing, summarizing, filtering, and expanding at one level, and by attaching meaning, context, and inference at another level.

Chapter 2 presented the detailed description of an information-processing model of CI. This model was developed on the premise that information flows through a variety of value-added processes in order to produce CI. While it is obvious that CI is related to a number of business concepts, it is a distinct discipline. The purpose of CI is to assess the various attributes affecting each player's ability to remain competitive in a given marketplace. On the surface, the processes involved in CI appear similar to those of information management; however, when CI is deconstructed, it is possible to see that the CI process goes beyond the information management model by performing the activity of analysis. Analysis is by far the most difficult and complex component within the process of CI, but it is also the one that adds the most value. Analysis is the heart of intelligence creation because it is the step at which information is transmuted into intelligence. The comprehensive model of CI presented here takes into account all of the values added through information management activities, as well as those added through analysis.

Chapter 3 went one step further, detailing the value-added processes involved in CI and discussing the nature of the values that a CI system should add to information. The value-added processes have been assigned both user and value criteria based on Taylor's framework (1986). This offers insight into the types of values that can be added through the CI cycle. For instance, when the CI evaluation criteria were mapped to Taylor's values, it was found that a number of values added to information through technology: closeness to problem, precision, selectivity, interfacing, linkage, currency, access, ordering, comprehensiveness, validity, simplicity, and flexibility. Among these values, those related to noise reduction contribute to CI throughout its entire cycle. Moreover, the values of precision and selectivity are fundamental because they can ensure the acquisition, organization, and retrieval of relevant data and information—in other words, the raw material—in order to create intelligence.

Chapter 4 examined CI-related technologies from a broad perspective. An amazing diversity of products are now available to businesses as solutions to information-related problems and challenges. Wading through the array of software packages can be a daunting task. A typology of software technologies helps to clarify the role that some of the products marketed for CI play in the process. The categories presented in the typology are based on the model of CI discussed in previous chapters, and serve to distinguish software tools that perform specific CI-related activities from those products that offer comprehensive solutions for managing the CI cycle.

CI software is changing and evolving at a rapid rate, and it is impossible for any product evaluation to remain relevant for long. A comprehensive set of criteria to evaluate new and upgraded software applications has been presented here for the first time anywhere, to our knowledge—certainly for the first time in any book. Until now, most published software evaluations have not made public the criteria used, nor were the criteria explained and justified. We do not claim that the 32 criteria presented here represent the *only* factors by which software should be evaluated, but we believe they express the dimensions by which one can judge the ability of a software package to perform CI.

Chapter 5 described the features of six software packages that offer comprehensive solutions for managing the CI process, four of which were evaluated using the criteria outlined in the previous chapter. The goal was not to rank the software packages, because they are all quite different, but to appreciate the extent to which these systems were useful in producing intelligence. Although it is easy to talk about value-added information within a system, it is far more complex to identify the steps through which such value can be obtained. And, once the steps are identified, the actual evaluation of software products is a difficult and time-consuming process.

The strengths and weaknesses of the software packages we studied were identified according to each step in the CI model presented in Chapter 3. All of the applications evaluated were found to add a number of values to information throughout the CI cycle, with the exception of the analysis step where the applications fared poorly. Bear in mind that our evaluations of specific CI-related process capabilities in the products we tested have significant limitations because, first, the versions provided to us were typically demos rather than full function versions, and, second, the software was not tested in actual corporate use. We were able to assess the overall strengths and weaknesses of the products and establish the values, in Taylor's terms, that they are able to address as well as the types of value-added capabilities they provide. The products met, in the best cases, 60 percent of our evaluation criteria, or 18 criteria out of 32.

Some valid conclusions can be drawn from these particular evaluations. Certainly, additional value-added processes could be integrated into the tested products given the capabilities of current technologies. The manufacturers might consider forming partnerships with established software companies in order to promote greater integration of existing tools rather than developing new and unfamiliar features of their own. In addition, as the software applications performed poorly in the analysis step, manufacturers might improve them by incorporating apposite attributes of expert systems.

All of these chapters have supported the notion that today's business world is complex, that creating intelligence is a sophisticated process, and that the marketplace for technology is constantly evolving to address larger and more complicated issues. The comparative assessment of CI software conducted here confirms the many ways of conceptualizing CI activities and outlines the contribution that can be made by CI software. The potential for technology to contribute to CI, although interesting, is quite varied. The dilemma for software producers is that, on one hand, to sell their products requires that they be marketed as simple to implement, adaptable to the needs of CI clients, easy to manage, and quick to bring a return on investment; while, on the other hand, the CI community recognizes that CI is a challenging process that requires a great deal of expertise and effort. Indeed, it remains unclear what role CI technology is expected to play in the sophisticated, information-driven businesses of today. Is it to replace existing CI practices, or to support them? Is it to educate end users, or rather to entice them into contracting new CI services and training? Is it to contribute to help business people become more adept at monitoring competition, or to eliminate as much as possible the need for human input? These questions remain unanswered, and we believe that they must be addressed by CI software producers.

In terms of the tasks executed by current CI technology, the question remains as to why so little attention is paid to the needs of CI client communities. Similarly, it seems odd to us that such a great emphasis is placed on the acquisition of external information while little or no attempt is made to address the problem of information overload. Moreover, one wonders how information can be acquired effectively without a strong understanding on the part of system administrators of the information requirements inherent in CI.

It is not surprising to us that analysis, the most important step of CI, is not addressed well in the current crop of software solutions, as this area continues to require a high level of human involvement. Artificial intelligence (AI) technologies are likely to be applied to the analysis function in CI in the future. As this occurs, CI manufacturers will have to reconsider marketing their products as "easy to use," as AI systems are difficult to install and require significant training for users. In addition, because AI systems are costly, many companies may be reluctant to invest in new CI applications. In the end, the technology will evolve if there is a market to support it.

Companies developing CI technology as stand-alone products are facing another major strategic challenge. Clearly, many technologies—not only information technologies—are converging as applications are integrated to achieve a vast array of tasks. Some of the software applications that we examined here are moving in this direction. They can be linked to other products and platforms and become interoperable with the information architecture of organizations. This functionality makes a lot of sense from a technological point of view. However, the implications may be that the administration of the CI system will become more centralized, in turn, taking the technology one step farther away from the specialized CI-related information requirements and needs. Eventually, systems may expand to handle an array of tasks, just one of which would be CI. CI practitioners would then comprise only one type of user, sharing the systems with many other organizational actors. Unfortunately, if CI experts are distanced from either the technological decisions or the essential means used to accomplish their function, they may be prevented from adding the greatest amount of value to information.

Adding value to information requires the selection of the right tools. Many organizations believe that giving their employees access to all available technological devices and information is a good strategy. Other organizations have learned, however, that they are not better informed simply because more people have access to information and technology—in fact, such access may discourage people from analyzing information and making informed decisions, which is the ultimate goal of CI.

In conclusion, it is fair to state that CI software has not yet delivered what the manufacturers claim. Although the products do address several aspects of the CI cycle, they do not necessarily make the CI process easier for the analyst. The knowledge base required to operate these systems effectively is quite large, and the management of CI using these software packages requires significant support in terms of administration and maintenance. Nevertheless, CI software products are still relatively new on the market, and we have seen some major improvements in a few short years. Given the pace of technological change there is no doubt that the future holds great promise for innovations in CI software.

Do-It-Yourself Evaluation Form for CI Software

Does the software...			Does the software...		
1. Help to identify the main CI client communities?	Y	N	18. Allow for hierarchical linking?	Y	N
2. Help to identify the CI topics?	Y	N	19. Allow for cross-topic linking?	Y	N
3. Help to identify the pieces of information required to address the CI topic?	Y	N	20. Store a variety of formats?	Y	N
4. Help to identify CI analytical techniques that address the needs of the CI clients?	Y	N	21. Store collected information as well as CI products?	Y	N
5. Can the CI topics and analytical techniques be changed?	Y	N	22. Offer an internal search facility?	Y	N
Identification of CI Needs Functionality—Score	Yes___ No ___		23. Allow for browsing?	Y	N
6. Help to identify external information sources?	Y	N	**Organization, Storage, and Retrieval Functionality—Score**	Yes___ No ___	
7. Help to identify internal information sources?	Y	N	24. Offer relevant analytical techniques?	Y	N
8. Relate information sources with specific topics?	Y	N	25. Allow for varying levels of analysis?	Y	N
9. Have the capability to monitor content changes within information sources?	Y	N	26. Synthesize (summarize) information in any way?	Y	N
10. Have the capability to monitor changes regarding information sources?	Y	N	27. Does the analysis result in recommendations for action?	Y	N
11. Have the capability to find specific pieces of information in particular sources?	Y	N	**Analysis of Information Functionality—Score**	Yes___ No ___	
12. Have the capability to filter information to meet minimum CI needs?	Y	N	28. Offer a variety of formats for viewing the final product?	Y	N
13. Have the capability to notify users about new information?	Y	N	29. Are the formats effective in conveying CI?	Y	N
14. Have the capability to import information in different formats?	Y	N	30. Can one format be easily adapted to another format?	Y	N
15. Have the capability to screen out redundant or repetitive information?	Y	N	**Development of CI Products Functionality—Score**	Yes___ No ___	
16. Have a function for rating the qualitative value of information?	Y	N	31. Offer a function for distributing intelligence?	Y	N
Acquisition of Competitive Information Functionalities—Score	Yes___ No ___		32. Help identify potential CI consumers in light of particular product?	Y	N
17. Offer an indexing function?	Y	N	**Distribution of CI Products Functionality—Score**	Yes___ No ___	

Abushar, S. & Hirata, N. F. 2002. Filtering with Intelligent Software Agents. http://www.engin.umd.umich.edu/CIS/course.des/cis479/projects/FISA.html [Accessed on October 10, 2002]

Ahituv, N. & Neuman, S. 1986. Decision Making and the Value of Information. In N. Ahituv & S. Neuman (Eds.), *Principles of Information Systems Management*. Dubuque, IA: Brown. p. 36–73.

Aker, B. 1998. An Information Technology Blueprint for Conducting Competitive Intelligence. *Competitive Intelligence Magazine. 1*(3), http://scip.org/news/cimagazine_article.asp?id=201 [Accessed October 10, 2002].

Albert, C. & Brownsword, L. 2002. Meeting the Challenges of Commercial-Off-The-Shelf (COTS) Products: The Information Technology Solutions Evolution Process (ITSEP). In: *COTS-Based Software Systems First International Conference, ICCBSS 2002, Orlando, FL, February 4–6, 2002. Proceedings.* (pp.10–20). Berlin: Springer-Verlag.

Atkinson, R. 1996. Library Functions, Scholarly Communication and the Foundation of the Digital Library: Laying Claim to the Control Zone. *The Library Quarterly. 66*(3): 239–265.

Austin, B. 2001. Mooers' Law: In and Out of Context. *Journal of the American Society for Information Science and Technology. 52*(8): 607–609.

Barclay, R. O. & Kaye, S. E. 2000. Knowledge Management and Intelligence Functions—A Symbiotic relationship. In J. P. Miller (Ed.) *Millennium Intelligence* (pp.155–170). Medford, NJ: Information Today, Inc.

Barndt, Jr, W. D. 2000. SCIP at the crossroads: A response to the President's message. *Competitive Intelligence Magazine. 3*(3), 39–42.

Bergeron, P. & Hiller, C. 2002. Competitive Intelligence. In B. Cronin (Ed). *Annual Review of Information Science and Technology.* Volume 36. (pp. 353–390). Medford, NJ: Information Today, Inc.

Best, D. P. 1988. The Future of Information Management. *International Journal of Information Management. 8*(1): 13–24.

Bevan, N. 1995. Usability Is Quality of Use. In Y. Anzai & K. Ogawa (Eds). *Proceedings of the 6ᵗʰ International Conference on Human Computer Interaction.* Yokohama: Elsevier.

Bouthillier, F. & Shearer, K. 2001a. Comparative Analysis of Competitive Intelligence Software Applications: An Examination of Some Value-Added Process. In Campbell, Grant D. (Ed). *Beyond the Web: Technologies, Knowledge and People. Proceedings of the 29th Annual Conference of the Canadian Association for Information Science - Université Laval, Québec.* 27–29 May 2001. pp. 341–352.

Bouthillier, F. & Shearer, K. 2001b. Étude comparative des systèmes de veille concurrentielle en regard du traitement de l'information. *Filtrage et résumé automatique de l'information sur les réseaux.* 3ième Congrès International Society for Knowledge Organization, Chapitre français, Université de Nanterre, Paris X, sous la direction de Stéphane Chaudiron et Christian Fluhr. 5–6 juillet 2001. pp. 265–273.

Bouthillier, F. & Shearer, K. 2002. Understanding Knowledge Management and Information Management: The Need for an Empirical Perspective. *Information Research: An International Electronic Journal. 8*(1). http://InformationR.net/ir.

Breeding, B. 2000. CI and KM Convergence: A Case Study at Shell Services International. *Competitive Intelligence Review. 11*(4): 12–24.

Bulger, N. 2001. Integrating CI with Strategic Market Planning through the Use of "Channels-To-Markets Mapping". *Competitive Intelligence Review. 12*(4): 39–50.

Calof, J. L. 1999. Teaching CI: Opportunities and Needs. *Competitive Intelligence Magazine. 2*(4): 28–31.

Carney, D. J. & Wallnau, K. C. 1998. A Basis for the Evaluation of Commercial Software. *Information and Software Technology. 40*(14): 851–860.

Castells, P. E., Salvador, M. R., & Bosch, R. M. 2000. Technology Mapping Business Strategy and Market Opportunities. *Competitive Intelligence Review. 11*(1):46–57.

Central Intelligence Agency. 2001. The Intelligence Cycle. *Factbook on Intelligence.* Washington, DC: CIA. http://www.odci.gov/cia/publications/facttell/intcycle.htm [Accessed August 1, 2002].

Chen, H., Chau, M., & Zeng, D. 2002. CI Spider: A Tool for Competitive Intelligence on the Web. *Decision Support Systems. 34*: 1–17.

Choo, C. W. 2002. *Information Management for the Intelligent Organization: The Art of Scanning the Environment.* 3rd ed. Medford, NJ: Information Today, Inc.

Cleveland, H. 1982. Information as a Resource. *The Futurist. 16*(6): 34–39.

Cottrill, K. 1998. Turning Competitive Intelligence into Business Knowledge. *Journal of Business Strategy. 19*(4): 27–30.

Cronin B. 1984. Information Accounting. The Use of Information in a Changing World. In A. Van der Laan & A.A. Winters (Eds.), *Proceedings of the 42nd FID Congress* Held in The Hague, The Netherlands 24–27 September, 1984. Amsterdam: Elsevier: 409–416.

Cronin, B. 2000. Strategic Intelligence and Networked Business. *Journal of Information Science. 26*: 133–138.

Davenport, T. H. 1993. *Process Innovation: Reengineering Work Through Information Technology*. Boston: Harvard Business School Press.

Davenport, E. & Hall, H. 2002. Organizational Knowledge and Communities of Practice. In B. Cronin (Ed). *Annual Review of Information Science and Technology*. Volume 36. (pp.171–228). Medford, NJ: Information Today, Inc.

Day, G. S., Reibstein, D. J., & Gunther, R. E. 1997. *Wharton on Competitive Strategy*. Toronto, ON: John Wiley & Sons, Inc.

Dedijer, S. 1998. Competitive Intelligence in Sweden. *Competitive Intelligence Review*. 9(1): 66–68.

Dervitsiotis, K. N. 1999. How to Attain and Sustain Excellence with Performance-Based Process Management. *Total Quality Management*. 10(3): 309–326.

Desouza, H. C. 2001. Intelligent Agents for Competitive Intelligence: Survey of Applications. *Competitive Intelligence Review*. 12(4): 57–63.

Dou, H. , Hassanaly, P., Quoniam, L., & A. La Tela. 1993. Technology Watch and Competitive Intelligence: A New Challenge in Education Information. *Education for Information*. 11: 35–45.

Dunlop, M. 2000. Reflections on Mira: Interactive Evaluation in Information Retrieval. *Journal of the American Society for Information Science*. 51(14): 1269–1274.

Dutka, A. F. 1998. *Competitive Intelligence for the Competitive Edge*. Lincolnwood, IL: NTC Business Books.

Eaton, J. J. & Bawden, D. 1991. What Kind of Resource Is Information? *International Journal of Information Management*. 11(2): 156–165.

Electronic College of Process Innovation. 2001. *Framework for Managing Process Improvement*.

http://www.c3i.osd.mil/bpr/bprcd/index.htm [Accessed on April 6, 2003]

Ellis, D., Wilson, T. D., Ford, N., Foster, A., Lam, H. M., Burton, R., & Spink, A. 2002. Information Seeking and Mediated Searching. Part 5. User-Intermediary Interaction. *Journal of the American Society for Information Science and Technology. 53*(11): 883–893.

Farradane, J. 1979. The Nature of Information. *Journal of Information Science. 1*(1): 17.

Favier, L. 2002. Mise en perspective des pratiques de veille d'entre-prises françaises à partir de l'utilisation des outils mis en oeuvre. In *L'information numérique. Actes du Congrès IDT/NET. Juin 2002.* pp.110–118.

Feeney, M. & Grieves M. (Eds.). 1994. *The Value and Impact of Information.* London: Bowker-Saur.

Fleisher, C. S. & Blenkhorn, D. L. (Eds.). 2001. *Managing Frontiers in Competitive Intelligence.* Westport, CT: Quorum Books.

Frishammar, J. 2002. Characteristics in Information Processing Approaches. *International Journal of Information Management.* 22: 143–156.

Fuld, L. M. 1995. *The New Competitor Intelligence: The Complete Resource for Finding Analyzing, and Using Information About Your Competitors.* New York: John Wiley & Sons.

Fuld, L. M. 2001. What Competitive Intelligence Is or Is Not! *Competitive Intelligence Guide.* www.fuld.com [Accessed on April 6, 2003]

Fuld & Company, Inc. 1998. *The Unclaimed Market: Intelligence Software.* Cambridge, MA: Fuld & Co. Inc.

Fuld & Company Inc. 2000. *Intelligence Software: Reality or Still Virtual Reality?* Cambridge, MA: Fuld & Co. Inc. No longer available online.

Fuld & Company Inc. 2002. *Intelligence Software: The Global Evolution?* Cambridge, MA: Fuld & Co. Inc.

Gale Group. 2002. Company Briefs (online database).

Gates, B. 1999. *Business at the Speed of Thought.* London: Penguin Books.

Ghoshal, S. & Westney, D. E. 1991. Organizing Competitor Analysis Systems. *Strategic Management Journal. 12*: 17–31.

Gilad, B. & Gilad, T. 1988. *The Business Intelligence System: A New Tool for Competitive Advantage.* New York: Amacom.

Gordon, I. H. 2002. *Competitor Targeting: Winning the Battle for Market and Customer Share.* Etobicoke, ON: John Wiley & Sons, Inc.

Gouillart, F. J. 1995. *Transforming the Organization.* New York: McGraw-Hill.

Griffiths, J. M. 1982. The Value of Information and Related Systems, Products and Services. *Annual Review of Information Science and Technology. 17*: 269–284.

Griffiths, J. M. & King, D. 1993. *Special Libraries: Increasing the Information Edge.* Washington, DC: Special Libraries Association.

Grzanka, L. 1999. Competitive Intelligence. *Knowledge Management Magazine.* April. http://www.destinationkm.com/articles/default.asp?ArticleID=726 [Accessed April 6, 2003].

Hall, C. 2001. The Intelligent Puzzle. *Competitive Intelligence Review. 12*(4): 3–14.

Harter, S. P. & Hert, C. A. 1998. Evaluation of Information Retrieval Systems Approaches: Issues and Methods. *Annual Review of Information Science and Technology. 32*: 3–94.

Herring, J. 1998. What Is Intelligence Analysis? *Competitive Intelligence Magazine. 1*(2): 13–16.

Hersh, W. 1998. Information Retrieval at the Millennium. *Proceedings at the 1998 AMIA Annual Symposium*: 38–45.

Hersh, W. & Over, P. 2001. Interactivity at the Text Retrieval Conference (TREC). *Information Processing and Management. 37*: 365–367.

Hocking, L. 2001. Applications of Competitive Intelligence. San Jose State University; San Jose, CA. http://witloof.sjsu.edu/ courses/282.willingham/CI/CIPaper.html#History2 [Accessed April 6, 2003].

Hoffof, B. 1994. Developing Information Systems for Competitive Intelligence Support. *Library Trends. 43*(2): 226–238.

Hoffof, B. 2000. The Information Technology Marketplace. In J. P. Miller (Ed.) *Millennium Intelligence.* (pp. 133–154). Medford, NJ: Information Today, Inc.

Huber, G. P. 1980. *Managerial Decision Making.* Glenview, IL: Scott, Foresman.

James, S. 2000. Focus on Global Competitive Intelligence. *Information Outlook, 4*(2): 43–46.

Johnson, A. 1999. Competitive Intelligence Software Applications— E-Business Focuses on Analysis and Integration for Actionable CI. Aurora WDC. http://www.aurorawdc.com/arj_cics_competitive _intelligence_software.htm [Accessed April 6, 2003]

Kahaner, L. 1998. *Competitive Intelligence: How to Gather, Analyze, and Use Information to Move Your Business to the Top.* New York: Touchstone.

Kelley, W. T. 1965. *Marketing Intelligence: The Management of Marketing Information.* London: Staples.

Kock, N. 1999. *Process Improvement and Organizational Learning: The Role of Collaboration Technologies.* Hershey, PA: Idea Group Publishing.

Koenig, M. 1992. The Importance of Information Services for Productivity: Under-Recognized and Under-Invested. *Special Libraries. 83*(4): 199–210.

Kurtz, C. J. 2000. *Business Wargaming.* Kappa White Paper. Laguna Hills, CA: KappaWest.

Lackman, C. L., Sabad, K., & Lanasa, J. M. 2000. Organizing the Competitive Intelligence Function: A Benchmarking Study. *Competitive Intelligence Review. 11*(1): 17–27.

Lang, E. 2001. Using Competitive Intelligence as a Strategic Planning Tool. CPA Consultant. *15*(4): 5.

Large, A., Tedd, L.A., & Hartley, R.J. 1999. *Information Seeking in the Online Age: Principles and Practice.* London: Bowker-Saur.

Liautaud, B. & Hammond, M. 2001. *E-Business Intelligence: Turning Information into Knowledge into Profit.* New York: McGraw-Hill.

Machlup, F. 1979. Uses, Value and Benefits of Knowledge. *Knowledge: Creation, Diffusion, Utilization. 1*(1): 62–81.

Machlup, F. 1984. *The Economics of Information and Human Capital.* Princeton, NJ: Princeton University Press.

Malhotra, Yogesh. (1996). "Competitive Intelligence Programs: An Overview" *BRINT Research Institute.* http://www.brint.com/ papers/ciover.htm [Accessed on April 6, 2003].

Marín-Llanes, L. Carra-Cartaya, J., & Espín-Andrade, R. 2001. Information Analysis Techniques for the Competitive Intelligence Process. *Competitive Intelligence Review. 12*(1):32–40.

Marshall, J. 1993. *The Impact of the Special Library on Corporate Decision-Making.* Washington, DC: Special Libraries Association.

Mass, R. 1988. Records, Words, Data …Whatever You Call It, It's Still Information. *Information and Records Management. 16*: 18–20.

Matarazzo, J. & Pruzak, L. 1995. *The Value of Corporate Libraries: Findings From a 1995 Survey of Senior Management*. Washington, DC: Special Libraries Association.

McGee, J. V. & Prusak, L. 1993. *Managing Information Strategically*. New York: John Wiley & Sons, Inc.

McGonagle, J. J. & Vella, C. M. 1996. *The New Archetype for Competitive Intelligence*. Westport, CT: Quorum Books.

McGonagle, J. J. & Vella, C. M. 1999. *The Internet Age of Competitive Intelligence*. Westport, CT: Quorum Books.

Meadow, C. T., Boyce, B. R., & Kraft, D. H. 2000. *Text Information Retrieval Systems*. 2nd ed. San Diego, CA: Academic Press.

Metzger, J. P., Palermiti, R., & Moriset R. 1998. Information Systems and Professional Activities. In W. M. el Hadi, J. Maniez & S. A. Pollitt (Eds.), *Structures and Relations in Knowledge Organization: Proceedings of the 5th International ISKO Conference*, 25–29 August 1998, Lille, France. Wurzberg, Germany: Ergon Verlag: 302–311.

Milani, A., Jr., Dou, H., & Quoniam, L. 1999. Where to Place Competitive Intelligence in Your Company? *FID Review. 1*(4/5): 19–26.

Miller, J. P. 1999. Some Competitive Intelligence Advice. *Information Today. 16*(7): 56.

Miller, J. P. 2000. *Millennium Intelligence: Understanding and Conducting Competitive Intelligence in the Digital Age*. Medford, NJ: Information Today, Inc.

Miller, S. H. *Competitive Intelligence—An Overview*. Alexandria, VA: SCIP www.scip.org/Library/overview.pdf [Accessed on April 6, 2003].

Mintzberg, H. 1994. *The Rise and Fall of Strategic Planning: Reconceiving Roles for Planning, Plans, Planners*. New York: Free Press.

Mitchell, K. D. 2000. Knowledge Management: The Next Big Thing. *Public Manager. 29*(2): 57–60.

Mizzaro, S. 1998. How Many Relevance in Information Retrieval? *Interacting with Computers. 10*(3):305–322.

Mooers, C. N. 1960. Mooers' Law; Or Why Some Retrieval Systems Are Used and Others Are Not. *American Documentation. 11*(3): *i.*

Morse, E. L. 2002. Evaluation Methodologies for Information Management Systems. *D-Lib Magazine. 8*(9): http://www.dlib.org/dlib/september02/morse/09morse.html [Accessed on April 6, 2003].

Nielsen, J. 2000. *Designing Web Usability: The Practice of Simplicity.* Indianapolis: New Riders Publishing.

Nielsen, J. & Tahir, M. 2001. *Homepage Usability: 50 Websites Deconstructed.* Indianapolis: New Riders Publishing.

O'Guin, M. C. & Ogilvie, T. 2001. The Science, *Not Art,* of Business Intelligence. *Competitive Intelligence Review. 12*(4): 15–24.

Oster, S. M. 1994. *Modern Competitive Analysis.* 2nd ed. New York: Oxford University Press.

Owens, I. & Wilson, T. D. 1997. Information and Business Performance: A Study of Information Systems and Services in High Performing Companies. *Journal of Librarianship and Information Science. 29*(1): 19–28.

Pirttilä, A. 1998. Organizing Competitive Intelligence Activities in a Corporate Organisation. *Aslib Proceedings. 50*(4): 79–84.

Pollard, A. 1999. *Competitor Intelligence: Strategy, Tools and Techniques for Competitive Advantage.* New York: Pitman.

Porac, J. F. & Thomas, H. 1990. Taxonomic Mental Models in Competitor Definition. *Academy of Management Review. 15*(2): 224–240.

Porter, M. 1980. *Competitive Strategy: Techniques for Analyzing Industries and Competitors.* New York: Free Press.

Porter, M. 1985. *Competitive Advantage: Creating and Sustaining Superior Performance.* New York: Free Press.

Powell, T. & Allgaier, C. 1998. Enhancing Sales and Marketing Effectiveness Through Competitive Intelligence. *Competitive Intelligence Revie*w. *9*(4): 29–41.

Prescott, J. E. & Gibbons, P. T. (Eds.). 1993. *Global Perspectives on Competitive Intelligence.* Alexandria, VA: Society of Competitive Intelligence Professionals.

Prescott, J. E. & Miller, S. H. 1999. *Proven Strategies in Competitive Intelligence: Lessons from the Trenches.* Toronto, ON: John Wiley & Sons, Inc.

Repo, A. J. 1989. The Value of Information: Approaches in Economics, Accounting, and Management Science. *Journal of the American Society for Information Science. 40*(2): 68–85.

Richards, T. 1995 A Comparative Evaluation of Four Leading CD-ROM Retrieval Software Packages. *Computers in Libraries. 15*(4): 70–75.

Rouach, D. & Santi, P. 2001. Competitive Intelligence Adds Value: Five Intelligence Attitudes. *European Management Journal. 19*(5): 552–559.

Rummler, G. A. & Brache, A. P. 1995. *Improving Performance: How to Manage the White Space on the Organization Chart.* 2nd ed. Toronto, ON: John Wiley & Sons, Inc.

Sandman, M. A. 2000. Analytical Models and Techniques. In J. P. Miller (Ed.) *Millenium Intelligence.* (pp. 69–95). Medford, NJ: Information Today, Inc.

Saracevic, T. & Kantor, P. B. 1997. Studying the Value of Library and Information Services: Part 1 - Establishing a Theoretical

Framework. *Journal of the American Society for Information Science and Technology. 48*(6): 527–542.

Sawyer, D. C. 2002. *Smart Services: Competitive Information Strategies, Solutions and Success Stories for Service Businesses.* Medford, NJ: Information Today, Inc.

Shneiderman, B. 1998. *Designing the User Interface—Strategies for Effective Human-Computer Interaction.* 3rd ed. Reading, MA: Addison-Wesley.

Sieverts, E. G. & Hofstede, M. 1994. Software for Information Storage and Retrieval Tested, Evaluated and Compared: Part 7—What to Choose, or The Purpose of It All. *The Electronic Library. 12*(1): 21–27.

Society of Competitive Intelligence Professionals (SCIP). 2002. *What Is Competitive Intelligence?* www.scip.org.

Stenson, J. Wilson, R. M. S., & Oppenheim, C. 2000. *Valuation of Information Assets.* Loughborough, UK: Loughborough University Business School Research Series Paper.

Sutton, H. 1988. *Competitive Intelligence.* New York: Conference Board, Inc.

Tague-Sutcliffe, J. M. 1996. Some Perspectives on the Evaluation of Information Retrieval Systems. *Journal of the American Society for Information Science. 7*(1):1–3.

Tao, Q. & Prescott, J. E. 2000. China: Competitive Intelligence Practices in an Emerging Market Environment. *Competitive Intelligence Review. 11*(4): 65–78.

Taylor, R. S. 1986. *Value-Added Processes in Information Systems.* Norwood, NJ: Ablex.

Taylor, R. S. 1991. Information Use Environments. In B. Dervin (Ed.). *Progress in Communication Sciences.* (pp. 217–255). Norwood, NJ: Ablex.

Vella, C. M. & McGonagle, J. J. 1987. *Corporate Intelligence in the Computer Age.* Westport, CT: Quorum Books.

Volpe National Transportation Systems Center, U.S. Department of Transportation, Research and Special Programs Administration. 1998. *Value of Information and Information Services.* October. http://www.fhwa.dot.gov/reports/viiscov.htm [Accessed on April 6, 2003].

Voorhees, E. M. & Harman, D. 2001. *Overview of TREC 2001.* http://trec.nist.gov/pubs/trec10/papers/overview_10.pdf [Accessed on April 6, 2003].

Walle III, A. H. 2001. *Qualitative Research in Intelligence and Marketing: The New Strategic Convergence.* Westport, CT: Quorum Books.

Wells, C. A. 2001. Analyzing Corporate Personalities: A New Method for Your CI Toolkit. *Competitive Intelligence Magazine.* 4(4):17–20.

Werther, G. 2001. Building an Analysis Age for Competitive Intelligence in the Twenty-First Century. *Competitive Intelligence Magazine.* 12(1):41–47.

Westney D. E. & Ghoshal, S. 1994. Building a Competitive Intelligence Organization: Adding Value in an Information Function. In T. J. Allen & M. S. Scott Morton (Eds.). *Information Technology and the Corporation of the 1990s* (pp.430–453). New York: Oxford University Press.

White, M. 1985. Intelligence Management. In B. Cronin (Ed.), *Information Management: From Strategies to Action* (pp.19–35). London: Aslib.

Williams, M. E. 2001. Highlights of the Online Database Industry and the Internet: 2001. In M. E. Williams (Ed.), *National Online Meeting Proceedings—2001.* (pp. 1–4). Medford, NJ: Information Today, Inc.

Wilson, T. D. 2002. The Nonsense of 'Knowledge Management'. *Information Research: An International Electronic Journal. 8*(1). http://InformationR.net/ir.

Yates-Mercer, P. & Bawden, D. 2002. Managing the Paradox: The Valuation of Knowledge and Knowledge Management. *Journal of Information Science. 29*(1):19–29.

Zhang, P. & von Dran, G. M. 2000. Satisfiers and Dissatisfiers: A Two-Factor Model for Website Design and Evaluation. *Journal of The American Society for Information Intelligence. 51*(14):1253–1268.

Resources

ORGANIZATIONS

Society of Competitive Intelligence Professionals
http://www.scip.org/

- Established in 1986, SCIP is the international association serving competitive intelligence professionals with over 3,500 members and 60 chapters worldwide.

- SCIP publishes: *CI Magazine* and *CI Review Journal*, as well as books, monographs, annual conference proceedings and videotapes.

- Main page provides links to services for members (information on events, peer networking) and a library where access is offered to *What Is CI?* and *CI Analytical Tools: How Effective Are They?*

AuroraWDC
http://www.aurorawdc.com/

- Aurora Worldwide Development Corporation is "a multi-faceted competitive intelligence outsourcing and support bureau, serving clients in every industry, with transnational primary and secondary research and analysis capabilities covering every continent worldwide."

- See http://aurorawdc.com/arj_cics_whatisci.htm, "What Is Competitive Intelligence?"

Richard Combs Associates
http://combsinc.com/

- A Competitive Intelligence consulting business since 1983, based in Chicago, USA.

- Site provides excerpts from guide: *The Competitive Intelligence Handbook,* which "provides an overview of how useful information is gathered and where it is to be found. This Handbook is a field guide for anyone needing to decipher the business climate."

Competia
http://www.competia.com/

- Competia is a "consultancy and training organization for senior executives and analysts in Strategic Planning and Competitive Intelligence." It offers a portal, a magazine, an academy, and organizes a symposium every year; thus it provides many relevant resources to CI professionals.

Fuld & Company, Inc.
http://www.fuld.com/

- In business since 1979, American-based but worldwide in scope.

- Provide sources to assist in the gathering of CI information: Internet Intelligence Index, CI Learning Center & Tools. See "Intelligence Dictionary" in *CI Strategies and Tools.*

Government of Canada Competitive Intelligence e-Monitor
http://strategis.ic.gc.ca/sc_mangb/cip/engdoc/ciem_hpg.html

- From the "Strategis" site:

"Keeping track of key players, emerging trends, economic conditions and ever changing regulations in a world constantly re-inventing itself is a challenge and a necessity for any Canadian business." … "*The Competitive Intelligence (CI) E-Monitor* provides you with pre-defined categories, keywords and syntax to make searching and finding the right information across a broad range of sectors faster and easier."

INFORMATION SOURCES ON CI

The CI Resource Index (also called CISeek.com)
http://www.bidigital.com/ci/index.html

- A search engine and listing of sites-by-category for finding CI

- Categories include: associations, books, companies, documentation, education, jobs, publications, software.

Intelligence Brief http://www.intelbrief.com

- "Integrates newsfeeds and references from over 2,000 sources, organized into 200 categories, all focused on providing operational, actionable intelligence to decision makers." See Intelligence for Business, Competitive Intelligence, and many other categories."

Brint Institute—Competitive Intelligence Programs:
An Overview http://www.brint.com/papers/ciover.htm

- This site offers definitions and a review of CI methods; the parent site (brint.com) is a portal for CI and KM.

Business.com
http://www.business.com/

- Business.com is a "business search engine and directory designed to help its users find the companies, products, services, and information they need to make the right business decision." It offers a comprehensive business directory where one can find links to various CI resources (linked to strategic planning) and useful business sources.

CIreport.com
http://CIreport.com/

- "The CI Report service provides focused, organized information resources for competitive intelligence professionals. Its first product, Internet CI, is an annual subscription available through the Society of Competitive Intelligence Professionals (www.scip.org) and includes the e-mail newsletter Internet CI Alert." Its developer is Bonnie Hohhof, a well-known competitive intelligence professional.

France Bouthillier

France Bouthillier holds a Ph.D. in information studies and has taught at McGill University in the area of management and business information since 1992. Previously she worked as a consultant in management and as a trainer. Her clients included large organizations (Montreal Stock Exchange, Standard Life, Business Development Bank, National Library of Canada) and small businesses in the manufacturing and service sectors. She has published articles and proceedings in French and English on knowledge management, competitive intelligence, and management issues in library and information services. She is the principal investigator of a three-year research project on the information needs and behaviors of small businesses and their requirements in terms of information services.

Kathleen Shearer

Kathleen Shearer received her MLIS in 2001 from McGill University in Montreal, Canada. She has been a freelance Information Professional for the past six years and, as such, has worked with organizations such as Bombardier, Bristol-Myers Squibb, Government of Canada, National Library of Canada, and others. Currently, she is contracted as a Research Associate with the Canadian Association of Research Libraries and is involved in developing and implementing new models of scholarly publishing, as well as investigating the future of research dissemination in Canada. She is the author of numerous articles and a contributor to the book *Access to Information in a Digital World*, from the Canadian Library Association.

More Great Books from Information Today, Inc.

Super Searchers on Competitive Intelligence

The Online and Offline Secrets of Top CI Researchers

By Margaret Metcalf Carr • Edited by Reva Basch • Foreword by Jan Herring

Here are leading CI researchers in their own words, revealing their secrets for monitoring competitive forces and keeping on top of the trends, opportunities, and threats within their industries. Researcher and CI pro Margaret Metcalf Carr asked experts from 15 CI-savvy organizations to share tips, techniques, and models that can be successfully applied to any business intelligence project. Includes dozens of examples of CI research in action and a range of strategies that can help any organization stay several steps ahead of the competition.

2003/336 pp/softbound/ISBN 0-910965-64-1 • $24.95

Smart Services

Competitive Information Strategies, Solutions, and Success Stories for Service Businesses

By Deborah C. Sawyer

"Finally, a book that nails down what every service business needs to know about competition and competitive intelligence. Smart Services *offers competitive information strategies that firms can put to immediate use."*

—Andrew Garvin, CEO, FIND/SVP

Here is the first book to focus on the competitive information needs of service-oriented firms. Author, entrepreneur, and business consultant Sawyer illuminates the many forms of competition in service businesses, identifies the most effective information resources for competitive intelligence (CI), and provides a practical framework for identifying and studying competitors in order to gain a competitive advantage. A roadmap for every service company owner, manager, or executive who expects to compete effectively in the Information Age.

2002/256 pp/softbound/ISBN 0-910965-56-0 • $29.95

Millennium Intelligence

Understanding and Conducting
Competitive Intelligence in the Digital Age

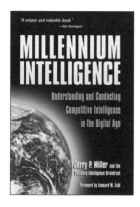

By Jerry P. Miller and the Business Intelligence Braintrust

With contributions from the world's leading business intelligence practitioners, *Millennium Intelligence* offers a tremendously informative and practical look at the CI process, how it is changing, and how it can be managed effectively in the Digital Age. Loaded with case studies, tips, and techniques, chapters include: What Is Intelligence?; The Skills Needed to Execute Intelligence Effectively; Information Sources Used for Intelligence; The Legal and Ethical Aspects of Intelligence; Small Business Intelligence; Corporate Security and Intelligence; ... and much more!

2000/276 pp/softbound/ISBN 0-910965-28-5 • $29.95

Naked in Cyberspace

How to Find Personal Information Online,
2nd Edition

2003 Competia Award Winner: "Most Insightful Book"

By Carole A. Lane
Foreword by Beth Givens

In this fully revised and updated second edition of her bestselling guide, author Carole A. Lane surveys the types of personal records that are available on the Internet and online services. Lane explains how researchers find and use personal data, identifies the most useful sources of information about people, and offers advice for readers with privacy concerns. You'll learn how to use online tools and databases to gain competitive intelligence, locate and investigate people, access public records, identify experts, find new customers, recruit employees, search for assets, uncover criminal records, conduct genealogical research, and much more. Supported by a Web page.

2002/586 pp/softbound/ISBN 0-910965-50-1 • $29.95

The Skeptical Business Searcher

The Information Advisor's Guide to Evaluating Web Data, Sites, and Sources

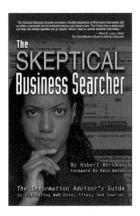

By Robert Berkman
Foreword by Reva Basch

This is the experts' guide to finding high-quality company and industry data on the free Web. Information guru Robert Berkman offers business Internet users effective strategies for identifying and evaluating no-cost online information sources, emphasizing easy-to-use techniques for recognizing bias and misinformation. You'll learn where to go for company backgrounders, sales and earnings data, SEC filings and stockholder reports, public records, market research, competitive intelligence, staff directories, executive biographies, survey/poll data, news stories, and hard-to-find information about small businesses and niche markets. The author's unique table of "Internet Information Credibility Indicators" allows readers to systematically evaluate Web site reliability. Supported by a Web page.

2003/softbound/ISBN 0-910965-66-8 • $29.95

Business Statistics on the Web

Find Them Fast—At Little or No Cost

By Paula Berinstein

Statistics are a critical component of business and marketing plans, press releases, surveys, economic analyses, presentations, proposals, and more—yet good statistics are notoriously hard to find. This practical book by statistics guru Paula Berinstein shows readers how to use the Internet to find statistics about companies, markets, and industries, how to organize and present statistics, and how to evaluate them for reliability.

Organized by topic, both general and specific, and by country/region, this helpful reference features easy-to-use tips and techniques for finding and using statistics when the pressure is on. In addition, dozens of extended and short case studies demonstrate the ins and outs of searching for specific numbers and maneuvering around obstacles to find the data you need. Supported by a Web page.

2003/336pp/softbound/ISBN 0-910965-65-X • $29.95

Web of Deception

Misinformation on the Internet

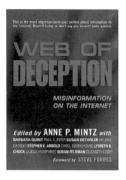

Edited by Anne P. Mintz
Foreword by Steve Forbes

"Experts here walk you through the risks and traps of the Web world and tell you how to avoid them or to fight back ... Anne Mintz and her collaborators have done us a genuine service." —Steve Forbes, from the Foreword

Intentionally misleading or erroneous information on the Web can wreak havoc on your health, privacy, investments, business decisions, online purchases, legal affairs, and more. Until now, the breadth and significance of this growing problem have yet to be fully explored. In *Web of Deception*, Anne P. Mintz brings together 10 information industry gurus to illuminate the issues and help you recognize and deal with the flood of deception and misinformation in a range of critical subject areas.

2002/278 pp/softbound/ISBN 0-910965-60-9 • $24.95

Super Searchers Go to the Source

The Interviewing and Hands-On Information Strategies of Top Primary Researchers—Online, on the Phone, and in Person

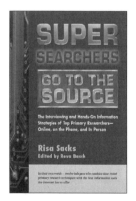

By Risa Sacks • Edited by Reva Basch

For the most focused, current, in-depth information on any subject, nothing beats going directly to the source—to the experts. This is "Primary Research," and it's the focus of the seventh title in the Super Searchers series. From the boardrooms of America's top corporations, to the halls of academia, to the pressroom of the *New York Times*, Risa Sacks interviews 12 of the best primary researchers in the business. These research pros reveal their strategies for integrating online and "offline" resources, identifying experts, and getting past gatekeepers to obtain information that exists only in someone's head.

2001/420 pp/softbound/ISBN 0-910965-53-6 • $24.95

For a complete catalog, contact:
Information Today, Inc.
143 Old Marlton Pike, Medford, NJ 08055 • 609/654-6266
email: custserv@infotoday.com • Web site: www.infotoday.com